PREACHER'S PROGRESS

PREACHER'S PROGRESS

by

DAVID IRONS

Regency Press (London & New York) Ltd.
125 High Holborn, London WC1V 6QA

ISBN 0 7212 0910 6

Printed and bound in Great Britain by
Buckland Press Ltd., Dover, Kent.

Dedicated to Eutychus, the man who dozed off during the sermon.
(Acts 20:9).

"Anathematising discourses . . . the would-be celestial pairs of bellows who blow their conceit at me."
Charles Dickens, *The Uncommercial Traveller.*

CONTENTS

CONTENTS Contd.

INTRODUCTION BY THE BISHOP OF BANGOR

No, not another book for sermons and preaching! If this short foreword can help to dispel such a reaction as this, then it will prove worthwhile.

I heartily commend *Preacher's Progress* emerging as it does out of a wealth and length of preaching and pastoral service. The author not only asserts, but proves, the importance of knowing one's congregation and of not preaching in a vacuum. True and genuine proclamation of the Christian Gospel, can only take place when he who does the proclaiming knows his God and knows the people whom he is addressing. This has, since the days of Martin Büber, been described as the "I-thou relationship". David Irons attempts to do for our day and age, I would dare to suggest, what Herbert Farmer did to illustrate this principle, when he wrote his classic meditations entitled *The Servant of the Word* nearly fifty years ago.

The reader will find instruction and edification from this book, but the pithy and racy style of its expression will also ensure that here we have a contribution to the preacher's library that can be *enjoyed*. It enlightens unwittingly and unconsciously, and this is the crucial hallmark of any good book or sermon for that matter.

† Cledan Bangor.

ACKNOWLEDGEMENTS

David Irons was encouraged to write this book by kind words from Martin Daly, the Editor of *The Reader*, following an article he wrote for the magazine, called *Proclaiming the Word*. In writing the book he received an enormous amount of help from Chloris Morgan, an award-winning professional writer with a distinguished literary background. He owes a special debt to the Reverend John H. Davis, Chairman of the North Wales District of the Methodist Church, who, by making it possible for him to serve in both Anglican and Methodist churches in this rural and bilingual area of north-west Wales, greatly enriched his ministry. Bishop Cledan generously gave up time and effort to support this book. David's wife and companion of fifty years also played a considerable part. To all these people he offers his thanks.

PREFACE

The title of this book needs no explanation. Everybody has heard of *The Pilgrim's Progress*. Its appeal is world-wide. It has been published in innumerable editions in at least one hundred and sixty eight different languages, since it first appeared in 1677.

The Pilgrim's Progress is a life story. *Preacher's Progress* will be slightly different. It will be like entering New York by train. The line leading to Grand Central Station has been underground. Ramps or escalators bring the visitor to the surface. He will find himself in Park Avenue and Forty Second Street, at the heart of a great modern commercial city. He will be ready to explore, and he will need a Guide Book. Even so, he will not see everything.

Another of the greatest books in the Christian tradition is by St. Augustine, and is called *City of God*. "Preacher" will be exploring a modern spiritual 'City of God'. After discussing aims and methods he will describe his arrival at the underground station and subsequent events. He hopes that others will profit from his experiences.

"Preacher" has had over fifty years of pulpit work. He serves as both an Anglican Reader and Methodist Local Preacher. He has made seven journeys of exploration; are we not told that God made the earth in seven days? And the figure seven occurs over a thousand times in Scripture! He tells us about his experiences under forty-four different headings; did not John Wesley also outline his message in forty-four sermons? In all humility, he is not a latter-day St. Augustine, or John Bunyan, or John Wesley. But despite his shortcomings, do come along, and join him in his excursions!

BEFORE WE BEGIN

Preacher discusses Aims and Methods

SERVING THE CUSTOMER

I have dozens of preaching books on my bookshelves. But in nearly all of them we are apparently practising our craft in a vacuum: they contain nothing about the listeners. Any preacher worthy of his salt will surely at the very least find himself discussing his sermon at the door afterwards. Sometimes he will receive letters. There may be differences and disagreements. Worshippers will wish to add little stories from their experience to what was said. He may be thanked for his helpful remarks.

I have, as well as my preaching, a connection with the tourist industry. My wife runs a small holiday business, and I serve on the Board of a company associated with the Wales Tourist Board. I am a tiny part of something which is competitive, world wide and vast. We employ highly trained experts, always active, who engage in what is known as 'Market Research'. We must know what the customer wants, and provide accordingly. There may be a little ideology about it. But the basic reason is that we want to be profitable in our businesses, and must have this knowledge.

With preaching it is the same, but our motive is quite different. We have to provide what is wanted. But we do it because the love of God in our hearts is calling us. We want to give back something of what God has given us; this is the way in which we feel called upon to do it. I have been called "Dai Windbag" (on television at that!); but if we are the sort of people who like talking, and are sensitive to the reaction of others when we do talk, then that is our scriptural 'talent', and we are told that we must use it profitably. But preserve us from becoming real windbags, bores who lack that sensitivity!

13

Over the years I have preached to innumerable people in dozens of places. I have a vision of a collective sea of faces looking up at me. It makes me feel extremely humble, for I know that many of those faces have belonged to saints of God, whose virtue puts mine in the shade. I know too that human beings are incredibly complex. Never jump to conclusions about anybody! I know that they have all come to church with a purpose. They want the comfort, the peace, the guidance that only God can give. They want to thank Him, and to worship Him. They want to broaden their understanding. They want to refresh their minds and spirits. It is my job to provide for their needs.

But heaven forbid that I should be sanctimonious, or even too serious about it all. Things can go wrong in church; let's have a good laugh sometimes! I remember a cat under the floorboards, which mewed periodically from different parts of the building (I wish I had a photograph of the elders at the Caernarfon church enticing the creature out with succulent cat food after the service!). I remember the day when I fell and broke my glasses; then, when I was hanging on to them trying to read to my congregation, my braces came undone. I remember the chapel where they had made special preparations for a Very Big Event. Unfortunately the newly varnished pews were barely dry, and it was not only the splendid oratory that kept us glued to our seats! Sometimes I have had desperately to avoid my wife's eye, for I know that if I do catch her eye I shall dissolve in laughter over some funny incident. I remember the Sunday when I announced a hymn, only to discover that the organist was asleep. I remember a congregation that was concentrating, not on me as I believed, but on a vase of flowers that was about to topple on to the organ keyboard. Once I shot the carafe of water over my congregation – and they happened to be Baptists! I once got hiccups just before a service; fortunately, it went, in the nick of time!

A minister friend of mine once had a 'customer' who demanded his money back afterwards! At least that has never happened to me!

On one occasion, as I was preparing to conduct evensong in a remote country church, I found myself joined by a woman in the still empty building. She came close up to me and, after a few preliminaries, said: "You know, I *like* men." What should I do? Hitch up my cassock and run? But then she said: "But of course you're not really a man. You're practically a vicar." So now we know, don't we!

But on a much more serious level, there are those times when God quite clearly takes over. I went to a church ready to preach on resurrection and life after death. At the very moment when we were singing the words of Job, "I know that my redeemer lives", a worshipper was remembering his young wife who had died exactly twelve months ·before. I once made special mention of a doctor in my congregation, not dreaming that it was the last time I would see him alive. These are just two of many examples. I think every preacher experiences those occasions when God shows His Hand in an obvious and uncanny way. The Holy Spirit is a reality.

My books of sermons vary considerably, and all preachers must read. Some are rare treasures indeed. The more run-of-the-mill books always contain at least some helpful features. The older books tend to be wordy and to contain a lot of padding. They date perhaps from around the turn of the century, when people were only too pleased to escape from their draughty, uncomfortable homes, and in the urban areas at least there were plenty of the new electric tramcars to take them to their destinations. People were less critical then, and the successful preachers of those days would make little impact today. These latter books have given me one or two occasions to smile. There was the chapel preacher who said that Sir Thomas More was a good man, in spite of the fact that he was a Catholic! There was the old treatise from the Scottish Kirk, which described in detail the evil ways of those who oppressed the children of Israel, and then said that they were just like the English! And who today would ever call a book intended for children: *For the Lambs of the Flock*?

But any sermon written in a book is a dead thing. One longs to see the preacher in his church or chapel, with his attentive, responsive congregation. A live, collective act of worship cannot possibly be reproduced on paper. But the bare words and the response can be recorded, and that, I think, is the intention of this book.

TECHNIQUE

Every craftsman, every preacher, develops his own techniques, his 'tricks of the trade', while not averse to learning those of others.

If I have a congregation that I know well, I sometimes try an experiment. I announce a certain text, from an obscure part of the Book of Leviticus, repeating it three times. Then I proceed, firstly with an explanation of the background. Secondly I define certain words used in the text, and then I proceed with the pros and cons of what it could possibly mean to us. By this time I can see the glazed eyes of a congregation that is not really with me. So with a change of voice I wake them up. This, I explain, as far as we know, was the only time Jesus spoke to a text. You see, the essential words in that obscure text from Leviticus were: "Thou shalt love thy neighbour as thyself." And Jesus started off with: "A certain man went down from Jerusalem to Jericho and fell among thieves." His questioners would have dealt with it as I had done, producing a pious talk without any impact – in fact, dodging the issue. But Jesus introduced a man who showed us how we should behave – one who belonged to a despised class of people. He was not a priest, he was not a Levite – he was a Samaritan, a heretic, one to whom Jews would not even speak. There was no getting away from the truth where Jesus was concerned! The Samaritan showed by deeds, not words, that he really did love his neighbour. It is the fundamental, challenging truth that lies at the heart, not only of Christianity, but of virtually every major religion.

Fifty years ago I was taught to preach as the questioners of Jesus would have done. The subject title, "Homiletics", was itself dated. The text and reference had to come first. Then I had to deal with it under three sections, to produce a so-called 'three decker'. I would accordingly find a text that appealed to me, but often its meaning was so obvious that all I needed was a couple of minutes. So I would pad it out under three headings to make it last a respectable time, incorporating perhaps a few polite little stories. I found my freedom when I abandoned what I had been taught. Now, although I discipline myself rigorously to keep within a reasonable time, I usually find myself with too much material – I use a broader base. Once I found a very old book of sermons that started off with a connected series of seven addresses. I condensed them into one sermon, and still had time to fit in more than the original, stripped of its verbiage, contained. But I write in all humility; I am inspired by good sermons. Sometimes I have listened to trained professionals who use the orthodox style, and I have enjoyed and admired what I have heard. I would be a happy man indeed if I possessed similar skills.

A sermon is not a university lecture. It *should* be interesting and instructive, but it *must* speak to the heart. And sincerity is absolutely essential; any lack of sincerity on the preacher's part will soon communicate itself to his congregation. Sometimes one has to tackle fairly complex issues, which some worshippers may not understand. There can be hazards: there was a little boy, whose successful ploy was to ask in a loud voice for the toilet, and there was a loveable but lonely old lady, who always had one of her funny turns when she was bored. A church is a family, and it behaves like one.

Children in church should never be 'patronised': their worship is as acceptable in God's sight as that of their elders, and I try never to ignore their presence. Much of what I have written will interest children; one section is specifically for them. But with regard to the most solemn and central act of worship, the Holy Eucharist, one must always remember that the Last Supper was a strictly adult occasion. Others may disagree, but I would never pressurise children into attending. If they attend, they must see it as a privilege. And young people beyond the age of puberty should never be treated as children; indeed, their devotion can sometimes be quite infectious.

Children obviously loved Jesus, and He must have told them many stories. We are told in St. Matthew's Gospel of how children interrupted a serious adult conversation about divorce, and of Jesus's response to His protesting disciples: "Suffer little children to come unto Me" – in other words: "Let them be, and don't be so pompous . . . "

The thirty-eight parables in the Gospels are, I would think, the bare bones of oft-repeated stories, stripped of embellishment. Much of what I have written is also bare bones, especially the section for children, Embellishment, the conscious play on the audience, will bring it to life. I think Jesus Himself would have been an imaginative, sensitive speaker. Sometimes He would have been uproariously funny, as, perhaps, with the farmer trying to count his sheep to check for losses (a worshipper in one of my congregations actually had a hundred sheep), or the woman turning the house upside-down over her missing coin, or the incompetent carpenters getting pieces of wood – the 'mote' and the 'beam' – in their eyes. Normally He would have been cheerful and smiling. Behind this outward appearance there would have been the loving heart, untarnished by malice, never retaliating. Gospel stories also tell us of His dealings with individual people. He always understood a person's needs, whether to challenge, to comfort, to encourage, or whatever. We must learn from His life, and with spiritual help emulate His ways. Sometimes He condemned outright, but with love. When He criticised the 'scribes and Pharisees' they must at least have recognised His courage and integrity, for they knew themselves to be powerful and dangerous. It would not have been possible to do Him justice through the mere written word. His would have been a tremendous personality.

Ideally (it is a two-way process) a preacher should play on his congregation's reactions *throughout* an act of worship. An invisible but powerful link will be forged. He will find himself responding to the devotional mood of his audience. The sermon will be embellished and flexible, there will be a strong sense of unity during the prayers, and the hymns and readings, imaginatively presented, will also form a part of the package.

I use visual aids when they are relevant and helpful. Stained glass windows offer the most obvious possibility; many other ideas will present themselves. But I would not go as far as Jeremiah, who smashed a jar in front of his listeners (Jer. 19:10)!

Journalists, radio and television writers, playwrights, story-tellers, novelists or whatever, presenting their wares in such gloriously competitive profusion, know that they must grasp the attention of their customers right from the beginning. Preachers must do the same. The man yawning in the back pew, the woman with a distant look in her eye, they are the targets! Children in the congregation can be useful; get their attention, and the rest will follow. And when one is conducting an act of worship the whole of it should be interesting. For example, eliminate superfluous verbiage. I have learned never to read out a part of any hymn that I am announcing; I just give the number. But I explain and direct attention to what it is that makes it fit in with my theme, perhaps also giving a brief explanation as to its origin. I also make sure that the congregations know and understand why I am giving them a particular reading. Sometimes I might give them half a dozen short passages with a theme, or just one passage, or connected passages from one book, or indeed any combination, with explanation. And I think we should lead our congregations at a reasonable well-prepared pace – no long pauses while we look for the page, for example! But a meaningful silence can also have its place.

Sermons, I think, are best delivered with no notes at all, and with the least possible obstruction between the preacher and his listeners. Some churches are designed so that it is possible to escape from the pulpit on to an open platform. I like to do so when I can. It is a matter of studying the geography of the place. A lot is sometimes made of the need for careful preparation. But paradoxically I would go further: it is possible to over prepare! I always remember the wise advice given to John Wesley just before his conversion. He was in a state of despair, even ready to give up the ministry he so much loved – of that later. But he was told:

"Purge your philosophies." His preaching was too complicated, he was actually trying *too* hard. When he learned to be simple he began to attract the crowds. Surprisingly, a straightforward story, derived from life, with a strong conclusion, can be enormously effective. But is it surprising? That is the way Jesus preached and He always made it simple.

Stories connected with people are always interesting. We can learn so much from the way in which others have coped with life's experiences. And we need background, descriptions of the cities or countryside where it happened and of the local political situation. This all makes any words which they have used come to life. And the stories need to be told with enthusiasm (I remember one genius who actually managed to read the story of the fall of Jericho in a way that made it sound boring!). Our subject matter can come from the present day or from any period or place in history, provided always that what we are saying has a firm scriptural basis which is completely clear to the listeners. Sermons based on particular hymns can be most effective.

At a personal level, I have been a broadcaster for many years, in the sense that I have run my own weekly programme on Hospital Radio. Most people could do the same. I have found that if one can speak in a natural and interesting way into an inanimate microphone, then gaining the attention of a congregation becomes much easier. I wish more churches had modern conference-style microphones, into which one can speak as one would speak on radio. One is able to cover more ground more effectively.

The rest of this book is the substance (or part of the substance) of the message I have attempted to deliver from the pulpit. It is set out in the form of an imaginary visit to a great city. "Audience Reaction" has been described where it is relevant. I have started with the most central and the most important, the vital highlights in the ministry of Jesus. In most of what I have written, readers will notice that I have started off by arousing the interest and curiosity of listeners. Occasionally I have wandered a little in order to bring in interesting points: I would not do that from the pulpit, as it would be irritating. The teaching, for which I am a mere channel, generally comes at the end. And the ending is clear-cut, with no repetition. Jesus set this pattern in His tale of the Good Samaritan, and prophets like Jeremiah and Ezekiel used similar methods.

MAINLINE STATION

Preacher arrives at the station – and here we must enter the spiritual realm, Augustine's City of God was not Imperial Rome, and similarly Preacher's City of God is not New York. Preacher comes up from the dark tunnels into the divine city of light after being pushed down and humiliated. Only then can God lift him up. Preacher speaks of this, and he speaks of the equipment he will need in his explorations.

THE ESCALATOR

I was once conducting an evening service, when during the opening hymn a young man in motor-cycling gear slipped in. He sat down near the back. After the service I went as usual to the rear of the church, to speak to the worshippers as they left. The young man waited. Then, when I was alone, he came up to me and said: "You know, I haven't the remotest idea what it was that made me come here tonight – I haven't been to church for ages. But do you know, it was providential! In your sermon you answered a problem that has been on my mind for ages. I'm glad I came." He described what it was. I said: "Yes, in my long experience of Christianity God often works like that. I'm delighted."

And indeed I was. Here was a situation that preachers dream about. I went home, glowing with satisfaction, and in telling my wife why I was late for my meal I enlarged on what had happened.

My euphoria lasted until the Thursday morning. There was a letter on the mat. I opened it. It was from a lady I know well, a devoted Christian, who had also been in the church that night. And gently, courageously, she told me in detail what had been wrong with the service, from before it started right through to the end. I writhed. Pride, as it says in Proverbs, always comes before a fall. I felt resentful, swearing that I would never preach in that place again if that was all they thought of me! But wiser counsels prevailed; of course my Christianity goes deeper than that. I knew in my heart that everything she had said was right. I had been unworthy. I accepted the rebuke in the true Christian spirit that I knew lay behind the letter.

And I turned to scripture, for one can always find analogies with our present lives in the old, yet timeless, accounts.

The story of St. Paul's missionary journeys in the Acts of the Apostles is familiar ground. We remember how on his second journey the evangelist crossed over from Troas into Europe for the first time, and his subsequent travels in which he visited various towns. But in each of them for various reasons he was obliged to leave after a short period. Then he arrived in Corinth. Here, as far as we know, he experienced his first real ministry, staying for eighteen months. It was a challenging but happy stay. After his departure he corresponded with his congregation. We have some of his letters preserved in the form of the First and Second Epistles to the Corinthians. Evidently they were a lively but wayward group of people.

But when Paul returned briefly to Corinth, the experience was devastating. Some person or persons during his absence had systematically set about undermining his position. He did not stay long. He went off, and sent them what we now know as the Second Epistle to the Corinthians from the tenth chapter onwards. Patronisingly, they had described his letters as 'weighty and powerful'. But in person he had no presence, and as a preacher he was beneath contempt. This, incredibly, of the great St. Paul! They had attacked him because he had not accepted any money from the Corinthians for his services; he would no doubt equally have been in the wrong if he *had* accepted money! He responded with heavy sarcasm: *"I never sponged on you. How unfair of me! I crave forgiveness!"* But perhaps the most hurtful criticism of all was to the effect that, unlike others, he had not known Jesus during His earthly ministry, and therefore lacked the authority which those others possessed. He hit back hard. These critics who claimed real authority were sham-apostles, crooked masqueraders resembling Satan himself.

Paul found himself 'obliged to boast'. Christians normally are humble people not given to arrogance. But here was an occasion when it was a matter of protecting and using a talent; scripture is clear on the point. So he described how he had been scourged, whipped, beaten and stoned, shipwrecked and imprisoned, how he had sometimes been face to face with death, how he had known toil and tiredness, cold, hunger and thirst.

And on top of all that, there had been his constant care for all the churches.

Then he gave his readers an intimate picture of himself. Fourteen years previously he had been 'on top of the world'. But more recently he had been afflicted with a 'thorn in the flesh' (inexplicably, some modern translations of the Bible have dropped this superbly expressive phrase). He had prayed to God that it be removed, not for the sake of ease, but because it was interfering with his ministry. God in His superior wisdom had refused, as He does with us all sometimes. And Paul, with his quite brilliant intelligence and insight where spiritual matters were concerned, understood. God's grace was all he needed. Power would come in weakness. He was to be well content, for Christ's sake, with weakness, contempt, persecution, hardship and frustration; for when he was weak, then he was strong!

That applies to me too. But unlike Paul, I deserved my humiliation . . .

To go with this story, there are some telling references to pride and its inevitable consequences in the New Testament, which preachers can use. There is the beastly moral pride of the Pharisee who believes himself to be superior to the publican, but stands condemned (Luke 18:9-14). There is the embarrassing pride of the status-seeker who seats himself on the top table, but is told to move (Luke 14:7-11). There is the short-sighted pride of the wealthy man who forgets that he is mortal (Luke 12:17-21). And finally there is the intellectual pride spoken of by St. Paul in 1 Cor. 1, which for all its cleverness fails to recognise the eternal truth.

THE BASIC ESSENTIAL
And so, to prayer. But first, some background . . .

I recently met a most interesting man. He was a Kurd (this was before the war with Saddam Hussein). He told me about his cold, mountainous homeland, sandwiched between the Soviet Union and the Arab States, Turkey and Iraq, an occupied and persecuted country. He spoke of Mount Ararat, eighteen thousand feet high, where Noah is said to have landed his ark. He described the excavations of ancient Babylon, with the remains of the famous hanging gardens and the place where the Tower of Babel once reached three hundred feet towards the heavens. We shared a knowledge of the Old Testament. But he, of course, was a Muslim. I tend to see the Muslims as being fanatical, but this was certainly not the case with him, for he was a moderate man (and perhaps some Christians are fanatical in the eyes of others!). There was an empathy between us. But in one respect he put me to shame. Good Muslims pray five times a day.

It occurred to me that it was about time that I preached again on this altogether fundamental subject. Consider for a start the Book of Job. Here was a godly man who could not understand why he had been burdened with a succession of terrible misfortunes. Surely his virtue deserved a better reward? Through forty odd chapters he wrestled with God in a form of prayer, until finally the answer came to him. The Lord lifted the captivity of Job when he prayed for his friends. Job's mistake had been his obsession with self. His so-called 'friends' had been insensitive and arrogant. They had hurt him deeply. But they were in reality pathetic creatures who needed his prayers. We make that mistake. People who hurt us are often in need of sympathy, if only we take the trouble to look a little deeper into their personalities.

There is a similar story in the New Testament. A man 'sick of the palsy' was desperately anxious to get rid of his complaint. Jesus could heal him. He put his prayers into action, by getting his friends to lower him through a roof to land close to where Jesus was standing. But Jesus said: "Thy sins are forgiven." Not what he was expecting, but Jesus understood that spiritual sickness was vastly more serious than any physical ailment. Jesus did heal his palsy, but this was of secondary importance. Again, misdirected prayer!

But this is just one tiny aspect of an enormous subject. In the gospel story we are introduced to a group of quite ordinary youths and men living and sleeping rough in the countryside of Galilee (for obvious practical reasons there were no women among them). Clearly they had all the personal failings one would expect, being touchy and quarrelsome, especially when they were cold and hungry. But they had with them another man, probably older than most of them. He was Jesus of Nazareth, perfect in His behaviour, always at peace with Himself, quite faultless in every way. They loved Him, admired Him, tried hard to emulate Him, but to no avail. But they had noticed that frequently, when they were only fit for sleep, He had gone off to some quiet place and had spent hours in prayer. Was this His secret? They asked Him: "Lord, teach us to pray!" He responded with the Lord's Prayer. But we can be certain that in private He did what they asked. When they were quiet together He would have shown them how He communicated with His Father, and how they could do the same. These men lived through the crucifixion, the resurrection and the day of Pentecost. They became the first wonderful Christians, the ones who founded the Christian church. Some of them made the greatest sacrifice of all by giving their lives for their faith.

Unlike the Muslims, Christians pray through Jesus the Man Who was a part of God. He it was who promised that He would be with us always, even to the end of the age. He is not remote like Allah, or the Jewish Jehovah. He is easy to talk to. He has the instincts of a parent, who cares, and He is with us, close to us, in the Spirit.

Real Christians organise their prayers very carefully indeed. They think firstly about Jesus. They thank God for the incredible sacrifice He made – for them, for us, who deserve none of it. They can only love back, and love their neighbours. Then, perhaps, they think of the needs of those neighbours. They pray for those who especially need their prayers, because of troubles in their lives, or because of particular responsibilities which they bear. In a way that we cannot understand, they know that their prayers do really help. Then, they might ask God to help them in their own activities, everything, even the seemingly unimportant. Then, probably they turn to themselves. We all know, don't we, that within ourselves there is a tendency towards evil. We bear malice. There is a silly touchy pride about us which affects our behaviour. We break the tenth commandment, although stupidly when we covet the opportunities or the talents of another, we only manage to harm ourselves. These and other failings are a form of spiritual cancer. They can destroy our immortal selves. All this, and much more. Millions of words have been written on the subject of prayer.

Scripture naturally helps us with our prayers. But if we turn to St. Paul we might be in for a surprise! In the Epistle to the Romans, Chapter 8, Verse 26, Paul writes: "We know not what we should pray for as we ought." Surely not – the great St. Paul, didn't know how to pray!

But he goes on: "The Spirit itself maketh intercession for us." Even with prayer itself, we need, we must have, the help of the Holy Spirit, if we are to do it well. Can you understand? Our minds may seem to wander (don't they just!) but the Spirit is there thinking our prayerful thoughts for us. I would indeed go further. When the Spirit is in the driving seat, then it is that we really pray in the truest sense of the word.

To carry this further, let us now imagine ourselves in eighth-century Canterbury, a quite different Canterbury from the city we know today. There was a beautiful, earlier, Saxon, cathedral. The monastery was presided over by an Abbot called Alcuin, who introduced the monks to the prayer we use so very frequently: *"Cleanse the thoughts of our hearts by the inspiration of Your Holy Spirit"*. Clearly it was based on the quotation above. We cannot lift ourselves out of ourselves. We need God.

And to go further still, it is always important that we should listen to the 'still small voice' which is the Holy Spirit. St. Paul's inspiring epistles came to him when he was 'listening', just as my best thoughts come to me at such times.

One worshipper, at least, must have responded to this theme – I received a rosary, anonymously, through the post.

THE GUIDE BOOK

I had a visitor, a doorstep evangelist. Reading from her well-used Bible, she quoted, from St. Paul's second epistle to Timothy, the words: "All scripture is given by inspiration of God." Did I believe this? "Yes," I said, "But what does the word 'scripture' mean in this context?" And I pointed out that at the time when the letter was written much of the New Testament did not even exist. She, I think, had intended to 'prove' by selective quotation and literal interpretation that orthodox church-going Christians like me were fundamentally wrong in what they believed. But since the New Testament was actually *created* by the Church she would, to me, have been irrational, as I would have explained.

Ordinary Christians need a basic understanding of what our present-day "scripture" is, without a lot of complex detail. It is our Guide Book, with the four Gospels at its centre ("Why four, when we have only one?", my Muslim friend might ask).

The Old Testament was written mainly in Hebrew. But some centuries before New Testament times many Jews found themselves in Alexandria and elsewhere where Greek became their language. They lost their knowledge of Hebrew, and scripture to them was the Greek translation known as the Septuagint. The Apocrypha, part of the so-called 'inter-testamental' literature written between about 200 BC and 100 AD, was also in Greek and is associated with the Alexandrian Jews. They seem to have been generally more liberal and pleasanter people than those with whom Jesus mixed in Palestine, who could be narrow, introspective and self-righteous.

The New Testament evolved gradually in Christian times. It is a complicated story. The earliest known reference to it in its precise present form dates from 367 AD, but it had mostly been in use from the second century AD. The leading churchmen who made the final choice were undoubtedly inspired by God, as had been the authors of the chosen books. Inspired by God, yes – but inspiration channelled through devoted but imperfect human beings. There is in addition a residual body of early Christian writing, some of it excellent, available to scholars, the work of the so-called "Fathers".

Until the time of Constantine, Christianity had been an often-persecuted minority religion. Constantine was proclaimed Emperor of Rome at York in 306 AD. Before the battle outside Rome in 312 AD which established his position he had a vision. Like many soldiers he was a worshipper of Mithras, the Sun God, in an exclusively male religion; but he saw, beneath the sun, a flaming Cross with the Latin words: "In hoc signo vinces" (i.e. "Under this sign you will win"). He believed, and the fragmented Christian church became a recognised imperial church. In 329 AD he moved his capital from Rome to Byzantium (or Constantinople). Two great Christian churches appeared, one using Latin and based on Rome, the other using Greek and based there. Conferences established questions of doctrine and dealt with such matters as the Canon of Scripture, the Greek version, and then the Latin version. The official Nicene Creed was also formulated, at a conference in Constantinople in 381 AD. It contains words from St. John's Gospel: "The Holy Spirit . . . Who proceeds from the Father" (John 15:26). The Western, Latin, Church later added: "and the Son", and the two churches squabbled for centuries about these three words. Christians today are sometimes like that; they make mountains out of molehills! At least, this was a doctrinal quibble, meaningful to theologians. Often the molehill is something absurdly trivial.

In Greece today worshippers, speaking modern Greek, still use with understanding the original of the New Testament and of the Septuagint, the Greek version of the Old Testament, which is quite remarkable. The Roman church has its fourth century Latin translation of the Bible, known as the Vulgate.

But whatever may be the technicalities, the Bible is beyond human description. Christians when they read it find it a perpetual source of inspiration and wonder; they grow in grace as their understanding increases. This book is based on the Bible. As a preacher I gain enormous benefit because I have to search it for its underlying truths.

But I commend the daily bible readings such as those offered by the Bible Reading Fellowship.

Of course, Anglicans have a supplementary source of inspiration, their Prayer Book. Apart from the obvious, there are many points of carefully considered detail, especially in the Holy Eucharist, which preachers should explain and share with their congregations. A small example in our Welsh book would be the thank offering: "All things come of thee: and of thine own do we give thee." These are words of David, quoted from 1 Chron. 29:14. And Methodism, we say, was 'born in song'. Methodists emphasize the tremendous spiritual inspiration that they gain from their Hymn Book.

FIRST EXCURSION. THE CITY CENTRE

Preacher starts with the great central truths, the Nativity and Crucifixion, the Last Supper and the Resurrection.

1. A ROMANTIC TALE

But this was no ordinary romance!

The young couple were deeply, deeply in love; it was beautiful to behold. They were setting up their little home, but there was a problem. A despotic government had decreed that they must make a seventy-mile journey. And the girl was pregnant and quite unfit to travel.

So they set off towards the south. The road was rough but flat. Mary and Joseph talked to each other as they trudged along. Wasn't this the place known as Armageddon? They spoke of the numerous bloody battles that had been fought there. Palestine had always been exposed to the north. To the east there was the protection of the Jordan valley, to the south, inhospitable mountains and deserts; and to the west was the sea. But, then as now, there had always been danger, from this one direction. The good King Josiah had been killed in battle there, so had Saul and Jonathan. They went on.

Eventually the track branched off to the left into the hills. Here was the ancient shrine and city of Shechem; and not far from it that deep, curious well, known as "Jacob's Well". Jacob (known too as "Israel"): that brought memories! And what a strange coincidence! Two thousand years before, Jacob had come there from the east. He had with him his beloved Rachel, for whom he had gladly toiled for seven years. Like Mary, she was pregnant. And they too were heading for Bethlehem!

Joseph and Mary continued along the twisting mountain road, and came to a city set in a barren inhospitable place. It was Bethel. Jacob, as a young man, had been very foolish and had had to run for his life. After fifty exhausting miles, he had collapsed in this very place. In his restless sleep he had had a dream. There was a ladder leading up to heaven. Angels were taking his fitful, panicky prayers up into the clouds. They were coming back with the message. God still cared, although he had been unworthy. And God had a great purpose for him. With Rachel and his retinue that purpose had now been fulfilled. He was the tribal chief of God's own people. Jacob and Rachel paused there and paid their respects. Joseph and Mary saw simply a Chapel Royal, which now marked the spot where Jacob had built his altar of stones.

Jacob had lived at the dawn of history. He had acquired a second name, Israel, the name today of a nation and country. Expressions such as "Jacob's Ladder" and "Jacob Sheep" are still in use today. Few men from the remote past have left their mark as he has.

Mary and Joseph continued. Soon they were in Jerusalem. Only another six weary miles to go . . . For Jacob this had been just a pagan Jebusite city of no importance. But, later on, David, Joseph's ancestor, had made it God's Holy City. Now, it was full of people, children, animals, stalls, chaotic in its overcrowding. But isn't it strange that probably nobody even remembered seeing that weary, exhausted young couple, with the baby so near, the One Who was to be the Saviour of mankind?

They trudged on. And then . . . they were nearly there. A hamlet, with a chilling name, a mile from Bethlehem. It was "Rachel's Tomb"! The two remembered how the beloved Rachel had died giving birth to Benjamin, leaving Jacob to live on into a lonely unhappy old age. What tragedy! We can only imagine what Joseph thought! (And it is most important here that any children present should be told that ladies nowadays do not die when they have babies; in those days there were no proper doctors.)

They reached Bethlehem. As a distraction they might have looked for the field where the boy David had tended Jesse's sheep. We know what happened there so very well – or do we? Thousands of Nativity Plays are performed every Christmas. They are warm and cosy, and the players are beautifully attired. They combine the stories told in Matthew and Luke, with the shepherds and astrologers meeting around the crib. Even the familiar words: "There was no room at the Inn" (Luke 2:7) are doubtful – the text could read: "There was nowhere to put a baby in the guest room." But above all the *atmosphere* is wrong. The truth, I firmly believe, is that the Son of God was born in primitive and shameful conditions, with the apparent stigma of conception outside wedlock. "He made Himself of no reputation" (Philippians 2:7). As with the crucifixion, it was mankind with its nasty ways, and not the Creator, which was really humiliated.

In Jerusalem, a week or two later, the young couple were back, fresh, well and supremely happy. They had their precious bundle, and they were going to take Him to the Temple. Inside they met a devoted, lovely old man. He took the Babe in his arms, and with prophetic vision exclaimed: "Now lettest thou thy servant depart in peace, for mine eyes have seen thy salvation . . . " He knew!

2. A HORROR STORY

This is the one archetypal horror story, from which all others arise. It is truly dreadful.

Reading the four Gospels, it is immediately obvious from their style and content that they were all written quite a long time after the events described, and that they are anything but systematic orderly accounts of the ministry of Jesus. It is also obvious that they contain gems of truth, and that these are fully sufficient for us to understand the wonder of the coming of the Son of God.

It seems that at the start of His ministry Jesus went to the hill tops above Capernaum, not far from His home in Nazareth. There, perhaps over a period of weeks or even months, He talked informally with groups of people. The account of what He said and did is what we now call the "Sermon on the Mount", or, in Luke's version, the 'sermon on the plain'. Thousands of words must have been spoken. We have these short summaries, or, if you like, selections of topic headings. Anybody who has ever attended a long meeting at which journalists were present, and has subsequently read the brief newspaper reports, will understand. Jesus concluded by telling His listeners that in their lives they must be like people who build their homes on the solid spiritual 'rock' of His teaching, not on shifting sand which will not stand up to times of trouble. Then, the comment is made: "*Jesus spoke as one having authority; and not as the Scribes.*"

Now the religious leaders of the Jews went through a rigorous period of training lasting many years. When people had problems to do with morality or anything of a spiritual nature, these leaders were the ones to whom appeal was to be made. But here was this extraordinary man, this upstart, interfering with their job, and apparently making Himself acceptable to those with needs! He must be stopped! Wouldn't we feel just the same? There was malice and envy in their attitude, but they couldn't see it. The bitter seed was sown. But oh dear, isn't this exactly how we would respond? Aren't these the thoughts that need to be cleansed from *our* hearts?

So the silliness started. The Sabbath Day for Jews was a wonderful day. Everything closed down; it was a time for the synagogue, for relaxation, for moral and religious refreshment. The carpenter's shop in Nazareth would be locked up; nobody would even mention business to Joseph or anybody else on that day. It was a marvellous institution. On one such day Jesus was walking with His friends through a cornfield. There was a song in their hearts. As they went they plucked the odd ear of corn . . . and the Pharisees noticed. They criticised – this was "working"! But worse was to follow. Jesus healed a man . . . on the Sabbath! How wonderful! But to them, this was dreadful; they held a council to determine how they could destroy this Sabbath-breaker! The spiritual cancer was spreading.

Jesus went on to raise His friend Lazarus from the grave. What joy He must have brought to the sorrowing village community! But the Pharisees, the miseries, met in council again. What were they to do? If they let this continue, everybody would believe in Him. And, they added, if that happens the Romans will come and take away our place and our nation. It was 'expedient' that He should be destroyed! Really? I think the only people threatened were the Pharisees themselves, although 'threatened' is perhaps not quite the right word. Such is the twisted logic of malice.

Then there was further trouble for them. The religious authorities in Jerusalem were involved in a financial racket on a large scale. It arose from the fraudulent exploitation of their position. Pilgrims had to change their money and buy birds or animals for sacrifice in the Temple. They created a monopoly, and then abused it on an enormous scale. Quite simply, it was robbery. Jesus interfered. This doubled their determination to destroy Him – and no doubt they rationalised their greed, as people do!

So these dignified, respectable men, eaten up with malice, tried to trick Jesus into saying that they should defy the Romans by not paying their extortionate taxes. He told them that they should 'render unto Caesar the things that are Caesar's' – they should pay up. And they actually poked around looking for witnesses who were prepared to perjure themselves in a Roman Court!

We all know the rest, and we can all fill in further details of the story. When Jesus was finally brought before Pilate we are told that he 'knew that for envy they had delivered Him'. Of course he did – Pilate was not that stupid! He understood human behaviour. Envy and greed and hurt pride and malice – it was going on all around him – as it is today!

Those Jewish fellow-countrymen manipulated the crucifixion of Jesus. But in this there is a terrible danger of misinterpretation. It is a matter of history; the Jewish race has been ruthlessly persecuted all through the years, because, it has been said, they killed the Son of God. Hitler went to Oberammagau for the famous Passion Play, and in the performance based on St. Matthew's Gospel he found his justification for what he did to the Jews. In fact the Gospel actually contains a text which would seem to justify Hitler's action (vide Matt. 27:25: "His blood be on us, and on our children"). Hitler would probably have even described himself as a 'Christian'! The true lesson is quite different. If we read the story through humble Christian eyes we see that those responsible for the death of Jesus were acting in an ordinary human way. It is a story that could happen in any community at any time in history. Indeed, when despite our prayers we give way to the evil tendencies within us, we are again crucifying the God Who loves us so deeply. His hurt at our behaviour is beyond anything we can imagine.

Here, let me tell you a story. A friend, a teacher of religious education, went on a training tour of the Holy Land. The leader of the party suggested that he had a chat with the bus driver who was taking them to the various places. This man was an affable and friendly Arab, who was obviously on the best possible terms with the Jewish hoteliers and others with whom they came into contact. He was a citizen of Jericho, with a mixed and interesting background, intelligent, and with strong views about the way in which the Palestinians had been treated by the Israelis. But going back, it transpired that he had been born in a village which had been utterly destroyed by Jewish terrorists. As a small boy he had been one of the very few who had managed to escape with their lives. Yet he could behave quite normally with Jews whom he knew. He did not identify the bunch of mindless thugs with the race to which they happened to belong. They were just simply – thugs!

Today we use the word 'crucify' to describe any situation in which a worthy person is unjustly treated. A year or two ago the papers carried the story of an elderly Archdeacon. He had been to the Centre Court at Wimbledon to enjoy the tennis, and had sat next to a teenage girl. He was old, and could not control his arm properly. Quite accidentally, his hand strayed and rested two or three times on the girl's thigh. A policewoman in mufti sitting behind him reported the incident as one of indecent assault. There was a predictable reaction. There were headlines in the less reputable newspapers. He was pestered by reporters and photographers. He was 'crucified' – by the modern press. He appeared before the magistrates, who acquitted him of a charge that should never have been brought in the first place. He behaved with great dignity, thanking them for their courteous behaviour (we remember another Victim Who behaved with a similar dignity at His trial). Then the Archdeacon wrote to *The Times*, explaining how all this had come on top of a desperately sad double bereavement, and how, in a strange way, it had strengthened his faith in God and brought him closer to his wife.

We do not nail our victims to a cross in modern Britain. We 'crucify' in different ways, with those responsible perhaps justifying themselves by claiming that they are fearless exposers of the truth.

3. BREAD AND WINE
In 1941 I was a naval rating serving in a British cruiser. We had been involved in a lot of action, the most recent being the *Bismarck* affair. We were anchored in an inlet in northern Iceland. We received orders to sail, and to our great surprise we headed north. Where on earth was it possible to go north of Iceland?

Our Captain soon enlightened us. We were heading for Spitzbergen; but where was Spitzbergen? It was a large island, we discovered, at the end of the Gulf Stream. We were to destroy the shore installations and to evacuate the Norwegian and Russian settlers.

It was a lengthy operation involving two trips to the far north, a long story which is not relevant to this book. Suffice it to say, it was light up there for twenty-four-hours-a-day, with the sun simply going round and round in the sky. The sea was as smooth as a millpond and the scenery absolutely superb, with the vast mountain glaciers sloping down to the sea. We went to within six hundred miles of the North Pole, and found that at such latitudes our giro compass would not work. But on completion of the job there were more serious matters needing our attention. Intelligence from occupied Norway had told the Admiralty about a German convoy which had set sail around North Cape with supplies for the front. Exact details were known, and we were to intercept. With another cruiser we headed south at full speed. And let us not mince matters: we were jittery. We knew that even if we survived the explosions, it would be impossible to live for more than half a minute in those bitterly cold waters. Our nerves anyway were on edge from our previous exploits.

The engagement took place in the half light of very early morning. For us it was a pitched battle at point-blank range, involving an enemy cruiser. From my action station in the bottom of the ship, with a series of vertical ladders above me leading through small hatches, I heard a sudden crescendo of explosions as every weapon on board was fired. Then a breathless Captain spoke on the intercom: "We have just sunk a cruiser." She had been so close that those on deck could see the men on board. For want of a better word, we 'won'.

Quite incredibly, dreadful events like these are sometimes treated as if they were competitive games or exciting adventures. They most certainly are not; they are sheer stark tragedies! The loss of life must have been appalling; but we were all right. When the same intercom had told us that the *Bismarck* had been sunk, we greeted the news in solemn silence. Our action was only a minor item of news earning an inside column in the newspapers. There was a German version, a British version, and the whole truth as we knew it. And it was *not* a matter of minor importance to those elderly women still living who remember that night when their whole lives were shattered by the loss of loved ones.

But it was what happened late the previous night that I want to tell you about. We carried about seven hundred men, and that justified a chaplain, a non-combatant who, like most of us, was serving merely for the duration. His proper occupation was as a parish priest in Kingston-on-Thames. Like all naval chaplains he played no part in the running of the ship and had no rank, although he lived as an officer.

We were at our action stations when we heard the message piped: "Holy Communion is now being celebrated in the captain's cabin." About *twelve* of us went. We were a group of very frightened young men. With our chaplain we ate the bread and drank the wine, recalling as we did so another similar group of young men who had done exactly the same in an Upper Room two thousand years before. We thought of the Leader Who was present then, the One Who meant everything to them at that time, and the dark clouds that were gathering around Him. We thought of the stories in Matthew, Mark and Luke in which we had been told to do what we were doing in memory of Him, and we thought of the later story told by John, in those five chapters in his gospel which amplified what had happened. "I go to prepare a place for you," Jesus had said, and then: "My peace I leave with you", the peace which passeth all understanding, the peace which comes from faith. We understood that we would not necessarily be saved from disaster. That was all in God's hands. But in the context of eternity God was in control. We emerged, not knowing what was to happen, but strengthened in our faith as the apostles had been.

On most Sunday mornings now, I am in my place in Llansadwrn village church for the Holy Eucharist, the title given to the Sacrament in the Church in Wales' *Book of Common Prayer (1984)*. As I kneel at the altar rail to receive the elements I invariably glance at the north chancel wall. There I see the tombstone (dug up from the churchyard) relating to the founder of the church and his 'conjunx', or wife. It is dated around 520 AD. Christians have been doing what I am doing in that precise spot through all those centuries. It is an awe-inspiring thought; and I know that through all those generations there will at times have been those with special anxieties . . . as I had once!

Ironically, I have met many Germans since those dark days; in particular, I remember two beautiful little girls who attended a Bible Class that I ran. So *these* were the people whom we were trying to injure and kill with our bombs!

I made this my theme for an evening service. I conducted the entire service without notes, from an open platform. I started with two hymns of thanksgiving, separated by a suitable prayer. Then we had the offering, and I explained that what followed would be linked together. I read Luke 22:15-19 (the institution of the Sacrament) and Luke 24:36-53, a post-resurrection passage, emphasising that it had all happened in a mere three of four days. Then we sang: "Break Thou the Bread of Life", and I told the above story. Then we sang: "The Lord's my Shepherd", followed by a prayer, the Lord's Prayer, and "Jesus is Lord of all the earth".

At the door, a lady came up to me. She told me about her son, a married man with young children, and of how he was desperately ill with a brain tumour. She was beside herself with anxiety. What could I, a mere mortal, possibly say? I only hope (and I am sure it did), that

Scripture had spoken to her during our worship, and that she would know, as we young sailors had understood, that God is still in control and has His purpose even in our darkest times. I told her this.

With Anglicans I sometimes ask my congregation to imagine that they are living in Rome round about 150 AD. It is the first day of the week. They are a persecuted minority. They gather together, probably in a private house. They now use the Greek word 'Eucharist' for what they are doing, having dropped the expression 'Breaking of Bread'. The leader reads passages from the 'Memoirs of the Apostles' and 'the Prophets'. That is followed by a sermon, a prayer, and the 'kiss of peace'. Then the bread and some diluted wine is brought in. Then after an extempore prayer of thanksgiving the bread and wine are distributed. The remaining bread and wine is taken to the sick, and, significantly, to prisoners (some members must have been imprisoned for their faith).

'Eucharist' means 'Thanksgiving'. At first sight it might be thought that the Last Supper as such was hardly a time for thanksgiving. But we are looking through the elements at the whole story of how Jesus the Son of God gave His life for us, completely unworthy as we are, was raised from the dead, and is with us always, even unto the end of the world. All that we can say, perhaps, is that any human word, 'Eucharist' or whatever, must be quite inadequate to express the wonder of it all.

4. ENLIGHTENMENT

At the end of his five wonderful chapters about the Last Supper, John tells us that the twelve men emerged reluctantly from the Upper Room, presumably in the early hours of the morning, and walked slowly out through the eastern gate of Jerusalem. In the half light the Mount of Olives would have appeared on their left, but in front of them was the little stream known as the Kedron. Probably they removed their sandals to paddle across. Today all one would find would be a dried up ditch, because of ecological change. Many of the trees in the land which Moses once saw as 'flowing with milk and honey' have gone, and many watercourses have gone with them.

We will break away from the story here, and follow the river as it then was. Jerusalem is set near a mountain top. To the east there is a four-thousand foot drop to the waters of the Dead Sea, two thousand feet below sea level, in its enormous hole in the earth. Nowhere else is there anything like it; it is the lowest place in the world. The Dead Sea itself is so thick with salt that it is like treacle, because the only way in which the waters which pour into it can escape is by evaporation. The steep mountain-side with its vicious rocks and gullies is hot and sultry. It is so dry that parchments such as those which made up the Dead Sea Scrolls can last for thousands of years. It is, in scriptural terms, wilderness country. The Kedron (the word means 'torrent') lives up to its name as it plunges down the slope; it has gouged out a deep channel for itself.

Around the year 520 AD a godly man called Sabas was looking for somewhere where he could live and meditate in peace. He discovered the Kedron gorge with its caves and its abundant supply of water. He established a monastery. It still exists; there is a road bridge nearby, and visitors can see the place, as they pass by on their way to Jericho.

Some two hundred years later, another godly man, tired of city life in Damascus, discovered the monastery and settled there. His name was John, and he had with him his little nine-year-old nephew Stephen. The boy spent the rest of his natural life, sixty years, there in that monastery. He was a man of God, a poet and a thinker. Reading the fourth Gospel, he came upon the reference to the Kedron, the river on which the monastery was so completely dependent for its water.

In his imagination Stephen thought about this in a sacred context. In a vision he imagined himself to be back in time and crossing the stream with those eleven men on that fateful night. He suffered with them as he witnessed all the dreadful events of the first Good Friday, the trial, the insults, the crown of thorns, the crucifixion itself.

But with hindsight he could go beyond all that, to the day of triumph, to the resurrection, to the day of Pentecost and to the magnificent lives of service of the Apostles. He wrote down his thoughts, in the Greek of the Eastern church. And that was not all.

Looking eastward he could see below him the deep valley of the Jordan and the Dead Sea. But across on the other side, on the mountains of Moab, on the peak known as Nebo, at the same level as Jerusalem, he thought he could discern the tiny figure of a man. It was Moses! The forty grim years in the wilderness were at last coming to an end, as Moses looked across to the land of Canaan, the land which he himself would never know. This was the land promised by God to the children of Israel. Stephen again recorded his thoughts.

During the nineteenth century, a man called J. M. Neale made a speciality of discovering ancient religious documents and translating them into modern verse. Much of his work is to be found in the

'Ancient' part of *Hymns Ancient and Modern*. He wrote "Good King Wenceslas". He also discovered Stephen's writings, and wrote the hymn which starts: "Art thou weary, Art thou languid, Art thou sore distressed? Come to Me says One, and coming, be at Rest". It will be familiar to many of my readers. It follows the Apostles, with a side-reference to Moses, through the nightmare to the triumph beyond. It is a question-and-answer sequence in seven verses. "Hath He marks to lead me to Him?"; yes, the wound prints in His feet and hands and side. "Hath He diadem as Monarch?"; yes, a crown, but of thorns. "If I find Him, if I follow, what His guerdon (reward) here?"; many a sorrow, many a labour, many a tear. "If I still hold closely to Him?"; sorrow vanquished, labour ended, Jordan past. And the magnificent climax: "Finding, following, keeping, struggling, is He sure to bless? Angels, martyrs, prophets, virgins, answer: 'Yes'!" The implication is that *our* lives follow the same pattern: with disappointment, with tragedy perhaps . . . but with life in all its fullness beyond!

After I had spoken of this in one chapel, a man button-holed me at the door. He said he was a Methodist minister on holiday, and that he fully understood. There was no need for me to ask further; the implication was obvious. He had a handicapped child by his side. I had only to imagine the bitterness and anger and frustration that parents tend to experience when this sort of thing happens to them. But I know too that, invariably, as the child, not quite normal in some ways, grows up in the bosom of a good family, the parents discover that he has something special, a rare affection, which others lack. He becomes a treasure in their eyes, a special gift from God.

5. THREE DAYS

I am now going to make another imaginative reconstruction, this time of a mere conversation. But it was highly significant. And it took place two or three days after the crucifixion.

There were three people involved, possibly a married couple, with a friend whom they met by chance. They began by discussing the Old Testament. Going back thousands of years, they spoke of a baby which was abandoned by the River Nile, near the spot where Cairo now stands. Even in those far off days, the Great Pyramids stood as they stand today. The baby was Moses. The "Children of Israel" had been utterly demoralised slaves cruelly exploited by their masters the Egyptians.

They had lost the will even to do anything about it. Moses the man tackled the Pharaoh. He led the Jews across the Red Sea. They existed for forty years in the wilderness. At moments of crisis they were miraculously saved, by water from a rock, by quails and by manna to sustain them. But more than that, Moses was a *religious* leader. The multitude would weakly have returned to their slavery. They had no fight. But Moses did not achieve his success in his own strength. He depended on God, and God gave him strength. He gave the people the Ten Commandments.

Then the three spoke of David. The Jews were now in the land which God had promised them. David, an unlikely choice as king, was the youngest son of Jesse, a farmer in Bethlehem. David created a capital high up in the mountains, like no other capital city in the world, making it God's Holy City, a symbol of the eternal.

And so they came to the prophets: these were godly men who gave spiritual guidance to the people against a turbulent background of historical events. But there was something more! Embedded in their writings was a promise: a Saviour, a Messiah, would come and would redeem them.

There was Isaiah, who said that out of the stem of Jesse (the father of David) there would grow a Branch, and the spirit of the Lord would rest upon Him. Unto them a Child would be born, and the government would be upon his shoulders. He would be called Wonderful, Counsellor, the mighty God, the everlasting Father, the Prince of Peace. But He would also be a Man of Sorrows, and acquainted with grief. He would make His grave with the wicked. He would bear the sin of many. He would be stricken for the transgressions of God's people.

There was Micah, who had said that out of little Bethlehem would come forth He that was to be Ruler of Israel. And there was Zechariah, who told the people to rejoice, for their King would come to them riding upon an ass. The war chariots and the horses would be cut off, and He would speak peace to the heathen. Despots who rule by force never last. Permanent lasting leadership can only come through peace and service.

The three could have continued for ever in their absorbing conversation; there were so many other mysterious words of prophetic wisdom. Only one person would fit the words: that was Jesus. But He was finished: He had died on the previous Friday. They were desperately unhappy. The third member of the group had joined the other two, and during the earlier part of the conversation had tried unavailingly to bring them comfort. But it really was all so recent, only the first day of the following week. Only time could even begin to heal the wound!

But while all this was going on they had actually been walking, following a spectacular path which took them diagonally across the mountain ridge above Jerusalem. They had walked seven miles, but they had no eye for scenery. And now, for one of them, Cleopas, they had reached their destination, his home near Emmaus. He invited the other two in for refreshment. Their new friend took the bread and broke it, and suddenly their eyes were opened. It couldn't be, but the manner in which He performed that simple act revealed His identity. They had had with them the Risen Christ Himself. It was true! He *had* risen, as others had said! And then He disappeared out of their sight!

It had all happened in a mere three days! At this point I produce a piece of bread and break it, and we sing James Montgomery's words: "Be known to us in breaking bread, but do not then depart . . . "

6. OVER THE HUMP

And now, to another resurrection story. But first, the background . . .

It seems probable that Paul and Luke first met during the second missionary journey at Troas in Asia Minor. Luke's narrative at that point begins to use the first person plural, 'we' and 'us' instead of 'they' and 'them'. I like to imagine that Luke was Paul's convert. I like to imagine them sitting there far into the night. Luke, the Greek-trained doctor, feeling that his life was complete but for one thing: he just could not accept the absurdity of all those Greek gods and goddesses! Here was a man who at last could give him the truth. The two men formed a rare and wonderful friendship. Paul was the letter-writer, while Luke set himself to writing first his Gospel, and then the sequel which we call (inaccurately) "The Acts of the Apostles". Imagine the day when Luke said to his friend: "Now look, Paul, you know what I'm doing. I want now to write about you. But what happened to you before we met?" Paul would have replied: "You won't like what I have to tell you. But if you are to understand me, it has to be said. I'm not proud of it, but you must write it down."

Then Paul would have told him. He was in Jerusalem at the time of the crucifixion. He had been at that time an arrogant, bigoted young man. He had persecuted the Christians. A courageous, noble Christian man had stood up to the mob, which he, Paul, by the very nature of his personality, had tended to lead. They had laid aside their outer garments. They picked up stones. They drove the godly man into a corner. They pelted him with the stones until he died. The hero's name was Stephen, and, said Paul, he had a face like an angel. He was a hideous, bloody sight as he lay there dying in agony, but he asked God in his final breath to forgive those who had perpetrated this awful crime,

This event should have made Paul realise that Christians had something which others lacked. But there is an obstinacy in human nature which made him persist in spite of the evidence. In a sort of blind fury he obtained his credentials for a journey to Damascus, where he planned to perpetrate further atrocities. But just before he got there, the resurrected Christ appeared to him. There was no possible escape for him now. This was proof positive. All the stories that people told were true. Jesus the crucified One was alive and real!

At this stage, those with no understanding of Christianity would say: "Well, what then? Paul must by now have been a broken, humiliated man. All that he believed in had been proved wrong. What did he do? Creep off and commit suicide? Or what?" But we know, don't we . . . this was acceptance of the loving, forgiving Christ, ready to rebuild the repentant sinner in His own image. Paul became, in his own words, a 'new creature'. He found 'the peace of God which passeth all understanding'.

Christ revealed Himself to Paul on the Damascus road. It was different for Colonel Moelders, an officer in the German Air Force during the Second World War.

As with Paul, his religion had been a religion of hatred. He was a Nazi through and through, a member of the master race, a killer. He had won a hundred and fifteen victories in the air. Then one day it happened! On a bitterly cold day, on the Russian front, he found himself being pursued by two Hurricane fighters. There was no possible escape. Suddenly he was afraid. And for the first time since his Sunday School days, in his desperation, he prayed. Miraculously, his prayer was answered. The living Christ came to him in that way! He landed with his parachute on the German side. But he was now a completely changed man, cleansed, forgiven and ready.

He confessed to a priest. He became a missionary in his mess. In conjunction with the Bishop of Breslau, he interceded with Hitler personally, saying that he (and others) wouldn't fight if the persecution of the Church continued. Somehow, he had to be liquidated.

So the Nazis put him on a plane, having first doctored the machinery. It crashed. He was killed, a martyr if ever there was!

Another vicious monster of a man was the victim of his own greed, for love of money is indeed the root of all evil. John Newton was the master of an eighteenth-century slave trader, living in the atmosphere of cruelty and filth which brought him his money. The Risen Christ came to him in his cabin, in the form of Thomas à Kempis' little devotional book, *Of the Imitation of Christ*. In this book the fourteenth-century monk with the help of scripture digs deep into the inward ways of Christ. In the light of his words even the most virtuous reader would come face to face with his own inadequacy. The rough tough sailor succumbed. Like St. Paul he became a new creature. He left the sea. He became firstly a customs official, then a curate in the Church of England. He wrote of his experience in the emotional hymn, "Amazing Grace". That in itself disappeared from most hymn books. But it had been set to a catchy American folk tune, and it suddenly found itself high up in the 'Pop Charts'. And the hymn itself became popular again. Such is the working of the Spirit of Christ.

I use the story of John Newton as the theme for a service. Firstly I read in abridged form, with comment, the stories of the wreck of the 'Good Ship Tyre', from Ezekiel, and of the wreck in St. Pauls Bay, Malta, recounted in Acts. We sing the Manx Fishermen's Song. Then to the extraordinary event itself, the evil sea captain, the slave trade, the monotony of life at sea in the Atlantic – and the spiritual dynamite in his cabin, the little book. Then we think about the Augustinian monk, and his seventy-two years of meditation, prayer and writing in his monastery in Holland, and of the central emphasis of his devotion, Jesus Christ Himself. We think about our own individual personal vision of what we think Jesus was really like. John Newton is converted; and we sing his most familiar hymn, the significantly appropriate "How sweet the name of Jesus sounds". From the reaction afterwards, I think any local bookseller stocking Thomas à Kempis' book may have had several additional sales!

A minor oddity about the story of John Newton is that unlike Matthew the apostle he sat at the receipt of custom *after* his conversion. Of course, men like Matthew were corrupt rogues and traitors towards their own people, whereas John Newton was merely making himself respectable by working for the government. I was a tax gatherer *and* a preacher myself!

But what a lesson all this is! I should like to record here three letters of mine which were published in newspapers. In each case the context is obvious, and there was no skill in the writing as such. The first two appeared in the *Liverpool Daily Post*. They read: "I lack the expertise of others who have contributed to the current debate about abortion. But surely we all know that mother love is probably the most powerful (and the most beautiful) of all human emotions. A confused, frightened young girl may take steps to destroy her child. But in later life the psychological effect of what she has done may prove quite appalling. I hope I can write this without creating hurt . . . " (15.1.88). (I had met a lady who had become a nervous wreck as the result of an abortion. She would wake up screaming in the night and was unable to bear the sight of a baby in a pram.) An expert writer responded to my letter with telling statistics about the psychological effect of abortion on women; and, on 28.1.88, I wrote: "Could I say a word to those women who are suffering from the aftermath to abortion. Before his conversion, St. Paul was implicated in many evil deeds, including at least one murder. After his experience outside Damascus, he became, in his own words, a 'new creature' and found the 'peace that passeth all understanding'. Perhaps he has a message for them?" The third letter appeared some years ago in the *Sunday Times*, as follows:

"Congratulations on your magnificent achievement in devoting half your Magazine to stress without saying a single word about Christianity! Over thirty years in the pulpit have convinced me that all the truths are to be found in Holy Scripture. Giving thanks for the many blessings of this life, learning that it is more blessed to give than to receive, enjoying the inward peace that passeth all understanding, avoiding anxious thought for the morrow, using one's humble talent to the full, loving one's neighbour as oneself, it is all there and much, much more. This generation is trying to live in its own strength and its failure is obvious."

In this latter case I received a most gratifying response; one deeply moving letter in particular came from Canada. Such is the power of the Press! The *Sunday Times* had closed its series of expert articles on stress. I also wrote personally and asked the editor to complete the picture by publishing something that would put the Christian point of view. He was unwilling to do so because the series was complete and finished. A pity!

I could quote many other examples. I believe we should use the media, newspapers, radio, television, as opportunity offers. In the near future, with the creation of hundreds of short-range Community Radio Stations throughout Britain, opportunities for preachers will be greatly extended.

I believe too that the burden of sin for those who try to carry it alone can be quite intolerable. A friend had a beloved wife whom he knew was terminally ill. During her last few weeks he did absolutely everything in his power to please her. Then she died . . . and my friend suffered bitter remorse . . . he could have done this, and he could have done that. His sin only existed in his own imagination. Only God could help him.

Paul goes more deeply into this question in his Epistle to the Romans.

7. SPECULATION

After his experience on the Damascus Road, judging by his Epistles, Paul hardly ever stopped talking about the resurrection! This episode concerns some who, foolishly, would not accept the truth to which he witnessed.

If Paul and Luke first met in Troas, and if Luke was converted to the Christian faith there, one wonders whether he had received his medical training in near-by Pergamos. There was a temple there to Asklepios, the absurd Greek god of healing, who taught that snakes crawling across a body could remove illness (that is why snakes are used as a medical symbol, for example in the insignia of the Royal Army Medical Corps). But paradoxically Pergamos also had a surprisingly advanced Medical School, with the first ever Hospital Ward. Whatever the truth may be, Luke was clearly a modest, self-effacing man, a delightful character, who wrote a quarter of the New Testament, more than anybody else. Yet he never wrote about himself! When Eutychus dozed off and fell from an upstairs window in Troas, the doctor obviously would have treated him. And when he and Paul were shipwrecked on Malta where they found much sickness, again the doctor would have used his professional skills. But Luke writes not a word about the part which he himself must have played!

If the two new-found friends conversed at length one wonders whether the talk was all in one direction. Luke, certainly, would have accepted with delight all that Paul had to tell him about the Christian faith.

Paul was such a gifted, intelligent man. Subsequent events, however, suggest the possibility that Luke may have responded by making a challenging suggestion to Paul. Why not go to Athens, the 'oxbridge' of its day, and tell the learned men there about the Christian faith? The story implies that there was some hesitation about making the short sea journey into Europe. A dream is mentioned, with the appeal: "Come over into Macedonia and help us." Dare one suggest that there might have been more to it than that? Could their ultimate target have been their generation of Greek philosophers, the current heirs of five hundred years of intellectual greatness unequalled by any other race? Were they embarking on a mighty intellectual adventure?

They made the trip, and stopped for brief periods at a number of cities. Eventually they arrived at Athens and arranged their meeting with the philosophers (who were only too pleased to accommodate them). The meeting was probably a long one (although the philosophers were people who enjoyed discussion, Paul's address in Luke's account can be read in less than two minutes!). Paul started with his reference to the 'unknown god'. The discussion ended when most of his hearers refused to accept his witness to the resurrection. In between he *must* have spoken about the crucifixion; there could be no rising to life again without a death first! My suggestion is that the difficulty arose when Paul failed to convince them about the crucifixion. They could not accept the idea of innocent, vicarious suffering for sin. After all, the Jews' own prophets, such as Micah, had seen animal sacrifice as being irrelevant to the godly life. "What doth the Lord require of thee," Micah had said, "but to do justly, and to love mercy, and to walk humbly with thy God?" Mohammed six hundred years later could not accept the idea. Modern intellectuals like Professor A. J. Ayer reject Christianity for that reason. Few of the Athenians seem to have been convinced. Some scoffed, we are told. Luke decided that, in his account, the less said about this particularly disappointing episode, which meant so much to both of them, the better. It was negative. He was under no obligation to record everything. I think the suggestion that the Athenians 'spent their time in nothing else, but either to tell, or to hear, some new thing' (Acts 17:21) comes from a disappointed man.

Paul, utterly despondent, would then have walked through the narrow walled corridor to Piraeus, the port of Athens. He would have taken ship to Cenchreae. Then he would have walked across the narrow strip of land to Julius Caesar's great modern city of Corinth. It was a busy road, with cargoes and even complete ships being transported from one side to the other (the Romans planned a canal, but that did not come until modern times). Corinth, unlike Ephesus in Turkey, was built in an earthquake zone. Consequently it has mostly disappeared.

Here he enjoyed, as far as we know, his first real ministry. It lasted eighteen months. Then he went away. He kept in touch by correspondence. In the first chapter of the first of his letters to the Corinthians he returned to the subject of the crucifixion. Clearly since leaving Athens his own brilliant intellect had been at work. He wrote of the Cross being 'foolish to the Greeks'. Did he have in mind those men of Athens who had scoffed at him? In a superb analysis he described how the foolishness of God was wiser than men. Faith is an experience that transcends the merely human intellect.

God's sacrifice of Himself is a unique feature of the Christian religion. It distinguishes it from the other world religions. It is what makes Christianity authentic and true. Paradoxically, although no 'miracle' was involved, it has always proved a stumbling block to the most intelligent people. It is not a religious truth that anyone would 'invent'. "Were the whole realm of nature mine, that were an offering far too small. Love so amazing, so divine, demands my life, my soul, my all."

In this connection, a friend of mine is a prominent British Sikh (problem . . . do I send him a Christmas Card?). Talking to him, I have found that the Sikh religion has much to commend it. It arose from a reformation within Indian Hinduism which occurred at about the same time as our own Reformation. Its principles come very close to those of Christianity; indeed I once conducted a service in which I deliberately chose hymns from the Methodist Hymn Book, on five different themes, which could have been sung with equal sincerity by a Sikh. But Sikhism lacks that one central vital feature: God's sacrifice of Himself, followed by His rising to life again. In his Epistles, over and over again, Paul refers to the crucifixion and the resurrection. These were, to him, the very essence of the Christian faith. Those three days were, to him, the most important in the whole history of the human race!

It must finally be made clear that the suggested background in this chapter is no more than reasonable guesswork. It is vital to distinguish between speculation and fact. I had a response from a worshipper who gave me a book, *Dear and Glorious Physician*, in which Luke is said to have been trained in a large American-university-style institution in North Africa. But I think my guesswork is the more likely!

SECOND EXCURSION. AROUND AND ABOUT

Preacher looks at some of the Parables of Jesus. He then looks at some of His deeds and words.

8. A SILLY STORY?

But the silly story has a meaning, as readers will discover . . . It is a Parable.

The silly story? Jesus spoke about an incredibly stupid man with a sack of seeds. He was throwing them all over the place, on hard paths, among stones, into thistles, such a shocking waste! Farmers, or gardeners, would be horrified at his incompetence. They would never do such a thing! A few of the seeds did take root and grow, but they were the exceptions. Why did Jesus tell such a story?

Of course, He was demonstrating a *spiritual truth*. With spiritual matters you never can tell!

The truth is that Christians must expect disappointment. But when we feel disheartened we must remember that it is God's work we are doing. It is His responsibility, not ours, if it goes wrong. Equally we must not take the credit to ourselves when things go well!

The Parable of the Sower is one of three stories which Jesus told about seeds growing. The inspiration behind them would be the Old Testament passages: "Cast your bread upon the waters, and you will find it after many days", and, "In the morning sow thy seed, and in the evening withhold not thy hand" (Eccles.11:1 and 6). To me this refers to the primitive practice of sowing seeds on flooded fields and collecting the harvest when the waters have subsided. But some modern translations apply the words to the export trade in grain. Young's literal translation seems to support either view. But that is by the way.

I was once, to my surprise, during the war years, appointed to conduct morning service at one of the enormous Central Halls which the Methodists built during the thirties. It had fifteen hundred tip-up seats, full cinematograph equipment, a superb organ . . . what a place! Unbelievably, I had a congregation of one! The place was a white elephant, a disaster – after all the love, all the effort, all the money! But that does *not* mean that the Methodists had been wrong to try.

An enthusiastic biblical scholar once had the task of organising the annual meeting of the British and Foreign Bible Society. He arranged a speaker. Then he collected together a wonderful array of Bibles in different versions and different languages. The evening arrived, the speaker delivered his speech and the people departed. Nobody looked at his Bibles, which he had spent weeks and months putting together. Again, he was not wrong in what he had done.

Again, during the war, I once visited a remote part of eastern Canada in mid-winter. In those days there was a railway following the line of the Saint John River. Romantic old-fashioned steam trains were still in use, with their cow-catchers and their hooters. Tiny villages with British-sounding names lined the route; the one I was in was called "Perth". To the north there lay a vast expanse of forest, almost unexplored, with bears and other animals.

In winter the river there is frozen over. The bungalow in which I was staying had triple glazing, with a thermometer hanging outside. While I was there the temperature one night dropped to forty degrees of frost. There was snow everywhere. It was so dazzling in the bright sunlight that the sky which looks light blue in Britain had become a rich dark blue. Children there are almost born with skates or skis on their feet.

"What on earth do you do with yourself in England with no ice-hockey?" they asked. A boy tried to teach me how to ski.

I made friends with the local Vicar. His parish was enormous. It included an Indian settlement, although in appearance the Indians were indistinguishable from everybody else. Then one day he invited me to go with him into the forest. We clambered into his large warm American car, and off we went, slithering along the rough roads. We arrived eventually at a lumber camp. These places can only operate in the winter when the tracks are frozen over, and they produce valuable hardwood. The men are tough. One of the wooden huts served as a church. And later I heard a story about one such place.

A priest had made his way with difficulty to the camp. He went into the hut and lit the candles on the altar. He waited. Service time arrived.

Nobody came. He waited a little longer. Then, dedicated man that he was, he went through his service in the empty building, and, seeing nobody, departed, a frustrated man. A waste of time?

Well, some time later, he returned to the camp. A man came to him, and said: "Do you remember when you came here and spoke to an empty church? Well, it wasn't really empty. I was at the end of my tether. I was about to take my own life. But I heard your voice, and I came to the door and listened outside. Something you said gave me courage. I changed my mind. I stood up to things. And my troubles sorted themselves out. Thank you!"

One afternoon a troubled clergyman attended Evensong in St. Paul's Cathedral. The choristers who sang Psalm 130 were probably hardly conscious of the words they were singing. But this clergyman was about to leave the ministry he so much loved. He too was at the end of his tether. And the psalm spoke to him. "Out of the depths I cry unto Thee" were words which led up to John Wesley's conversion that very evening, something which I shall talk about in greater depth later.

The boy scout, who in 1909 did his daily good turn by helping an American visitor to London, little dreamt that his action would lead up to the formation of the Boy Scouts of America. The American, a rich man, was so impressed by his refusal to take a tip that he went back to Chicago determined that the Americans too should have their boy scouts. Once home, he set to work, and the American organisation was created. It became enormous.

Jesus spoke of a tiny mustard seed growing into a mighty tree in which the birds could nest, didn't He. Just as it is nature's way to provide millions of acorns to produce one oak tree, so we Christians must be haphazard and prolific in all our good works.

If Jesus had been telling His story today He would probably have made His 'sower' a Christian satellite radio station like UCB (which is kept going entirely by voluntary subscription). When I talk about my faith in its studio (as I have done) my voice can be picked up anywhere in Europe! There must be good soil somewhere in that vast area!

9. TEENAGERS

Some sad family stories, which will lead us up to some surprising Gospel teaching, a Parable, in fact . . .

A business executive, of Welsh extraction, was delighted when one day he heard that he was being moved to new premises in North Wales. His family once again would be able to attend the Calvinistic Methodist Chapel. They would be able to sing the grand old Welsh hymns, and join in the Singing Festivals.

He had two teenage daughters, who both settled well in the local Secondary School. But after a while the older girl seemed troubled. After questioning they discovered the reason: she was pregnant. Honourable people that they were, they were unwilling to take the obvious way out. The child was born . . . and let us leave them there . . .

Another good family, this time living in England. Both husband and wife were keen Church workers, he a Churchwarden and organist, she a pillar of the Mothers' Union. They had a son and daughter, both in their teens. Their son was studying electronic engineering at University; they were proud of him. But the daughter? She had walked out. Just disappeared, two years previously. They believed she might be living in the slums of some great city, with an undesirable man. They had no idea . . .

Again in a different part of England. A bank manager and his wife, he a Rotarian, well known and well liked, she a prominent member of the W.I., and both active members of the Parish Church. They had a teenage son and a teenage daughter. Both seemed to have promising careers ahead of them. The boy hoped to become a chartered accountant. But incredibly, with some other sixth formers, he managed to get himself involved in an illegal practice. They believed that they had found a fool-proof method of defrauding a large public utility. Inevitably, they were caught. He acquired a criminal record . . .

My final story comes from the countryside. There was a prosperous, upright, worthy farmer, a widower, with two teenage sons, both of whom had money in their own right. One day one of his sons walked out, disappeared, taking with him all his money . . .

And now to the sequels. The mother looked after the new baby while her daughter went out to work (there was no recrimination). Then, surprisingly, the girl met a nice, high-principled young man, active in youth work. They fell in love and married. But the truth had to come out. He was a homosexual, only too pleased to find a ready-made family. One's heart bleeds for him and his natural condition which made life so difficult; but the marriage fell apart. And still they coped . . .

The girl who disappeared? Those two good parents would have given anything, anything at all, to hear that knock on the door. It would not have mattered what problems, babies, whatever it might be, the girl might bring with her. But the knock never came . . .

The would-be chartered accountant? The whole family rallied round, without recrimination. The past was the past. Of course with his criminal record the boy could never become an accountant. They found the capital, and they installed him in his own private business.

The farmer's son? He frittered away all his money on evil activities in the big city. Then, reluctantly, although he really had no choice, he returned home. The farmer killed the fatted calf. It is the story of the Prodigal Son! The elder son grumbled. But it is a fair guess that when they had settled down again, both father and elder son did all they could to reinstate the boy, without recrimination. One does wonder how a mother would have coped with these circumstances. But there was no mother!

These four stories are absolutely true to life. Sometimes we talk from our pulpits about family life, with the intimate complicated relationship between man and wife, something that has to be constantly 'worked at' if it is to succeed. We talk too about family tensions in a wider sense. There were even tensions in the Holy Family itself (read about the incident at the end of Chapter 2 in St. Luke). People have told me of their individual problems, with 'prodigal sons' and the like.

This particular story has a spiritual meaning. The farmer represents God. It demonstrates the way in which our relationship with Him resembles the relationship between a human parent and his (or her) child, albeit on a higher plain. Hebrews 12:5-11 describes how God disciplines us, just as a worthy human father disciplines his child for his own good. It is justice tempered with an abiding love. It is, for us, "growing", or "growing up", in the faith; and we all slip up in the process. In all these stories the parents continued to love their wayward children. They forgave, they desperately wanted them to live worthy and happy lives. God is like that.

Interestingly, the Islamic faith shares much of what we believe as Christians. The Old Testament is theirs as much as ours. They believe in Jesus as a great prophet, but not as the Son of God. They believe that He was born of a virgin, who was visited by the same Angel Gabriel who spoke to Mohammed. They do not believe that He was crucified. But there is one other fundamental difference. 'Islam' means finding peace of mind through submission to God's will. The Christian on the other hand sees God as being like a perfect human father – or 'mother' – with all the instincts which we associate with parenthood. The Parable of the Prodigal Son demonstrates our belief. I think a Muslim would say that the prodigal should get what he deserved and be punished. But our Christian God gave His life for His wayward children.

As I write I read of a swimming tragedy. A child disobeyed his father and went swimming in a river. He got into difficulties. Without a moment's thought the father went in after him. The father drowned, the child survived. He 'gave his life for his son'.

10. INVESTMENT

And so to another Parable . . .

Immediately after the story of Zacchaeus' conversion in Luke's Gospel, Jesus is quoted as telling a Parable about money (Luke 19:11-27); there is a similar story in Matthew. It tells how a master gave his servants 'pounds' (or 'talents') to handle while he went away. The one who invested well was praised. Of course it is not really about the Stock Exchange, but is concerned with spiritual assets. We must use our talents to the utmost; that is the message. Matthew has left us the superbly beautiful phrase, directed towards those who succeed: "*Well done*, thou good and faithful servant."

If you were to visit the tiny island of Bocas del Toro, just off the coast of Panama in Central America, you might have a surprise (I am writing of the situation as it was fifty years ago). You would find a Methodist Church, the Bank Church, and a Minister superintending a number of such churches in the group of islands. Six hundred miles away, across the sea, the Chairman of the District was stationed in Jamaica. The congregation would have been a mixture of races.

Sometimes on the island you would see groups of Indian traders, who had made the hazardous thirty-mile trip from the mainland. These were primitive people. The Bank Church was a good church. Hence, with true missionary zeal, they passed a resolution that their Minister should visit the mainland at roughly six-monthly intervals. For his first trip they hired a small motor launch called, jokingly, *The Titanic*. They got there, after some anxiety; the boat was in the charge of an utterly irresponsible youth with a rifle, who periodically stopped to take pot-shots at the birds. These occasional visits continued for about four years.

The 'Valiente Indians' were primitive indeed. Their 'homes' were no more than thatched roofs supported by poles; a sloping notched pole enabled them to climb up into the thatch at night-time. There were many dangerous animals around. Paths through the bush separated the houses. It was a society in which human life was cheap, in which concern for others was non-existent and in which women were chattels. It was 'savage' in the true sense of the word.

The Methodists of Bocas del Toro decided that something must be done about it. They wanted a full-time missionary. They approached London, and they approached Jamaica, but resources were not available. But something *must* be done! They looked among their own members. The only possibility was the irresponsible youth, who had certainly grown up and was now a member; but he had no education, no ability and was still immature. Dare they? The Minister approached him. He prayed about it. He agreed to go.

He was given the necessities of life, together with Sunday School pictures and a magic lantern with slides (but no rifle!). They even had trouble getting him ashore; he had to wade through mud three feet deep. But he got there.

The incredible story started with him befriending the numerous children and picking up the unwritten language from them (this in itself presented problems. They had several different ways of counting, for example!). He found food and a roof (a pigsty!). He taught the simple Gospel stories, using his equipment. Gradually through the years he built up an enthusiastic church. He married. He was ordained. But vitally the ways of the islanders were transformed. They became kindly and considerate. The vicious side was eradicated. Just as so many of the cannibals in the South Pacific were transformed by Christianity, so were these people.

I met the Rev. Alphonse in 1938 in England. and still have an autographed copy of his book. Today, fifty years later, his work continues, in a wonderful way . . .

Just as he used talents which one would say for him were almost negligible, so must we! *Well done*, thou good and faithful servant!

Five years later I met another great man in the missionary field, Basil Mathews. Older people may remember the many missionary books which he wrote and which were published cheaply in paperback form during the thirties. He was, during the War years, a Professor in Boston Theological College, specialising in world affairs. He was a great Christian, seeing the peoples of the world through sympathetic Christian eyes. His knowledge was vast. He understood and transmitted to those who attended his lectures all the ethnic, religious, cultural and linguistic problems which cause tension and conflict, and pointed to the way of love which was the only answer. He himself, an Oxford man, met with a particular racial problem in Boston; unfortunately the descendants of the early English settlers and of the later Irish immigrants do not see eye to eye, and there is unreasonable prejudice on both sides. Basil, in a sense, was glad to accept a new appointment in Vancouver where he felt the atmosphere would be more rational. I attended some of his lectures, and his farewell dinner. He is, to me, a precious memory.

With regard to missionary work generally, I can never understand why stories about missionaries and cannibals are supposed to be funny. There was nothing funny about those inhabitants of Pacific Islands who sharpened their teeth to a point and devoured human flesh because no animals were available. Some missionaries sacrificed themselves in a horrible way. Their overall achievement under God's guidance was enormous. Of course, there were some who were insensitive and arrogant; I cannot read the words of "From Greenlands Icy Mountains" without a shudder. But I believe that the present fashionable habit in some quarters of sneering at the missionaries is quite, quite wrong.

St. Paul was the greatest missionary of them all. He describes his attitude in his first epistle to the Corinthians. To the Jews he became as a Jew, that he might gain the Jews. He became all things to all men. He treated with respect and understanding the beliefs of others, knowing that that was the way to convince them and to convert them. There was love in his heart; without love whatever he did was worthless.

Members of a congregation once actually walked out on me when I prayed for the 'leaders of the other great religions of the world'. Yet it was a truly loving prayer which did not in any way compromise my own heartfelt beliefs.

11. HOLIDAY

We come now to a series of incidents in the life of Jesus . . . Between Spring and Autumn the Jews have three great Festival times. Each has a religious significance but is also related to agriculture. The first is Passover, and the barley harvest, the second, Pentecost, and the wheat harvest, and the third, Tabernacles, and the fruit harvest.

Imagine that we are attending the Feast of Tabernacles. The year is round about 30 AD. Great multitudes are heading for Jerusalem, the capital city, the families, the young men and women, the aged, all with their different forms of transport. The city is crowded. As soon as the people arrive, they build their 'tabernacles'; the children run around looking for branches of palm, myrtle and olive. These are sited around or within the city, even on the flat roofs of buildings, and will be 'home' for eight days. There is tremendous excitement. Gathering in the grapes and pressing them to make wine has been exhausting work in the sub-tropical sunshine (wine was the main drink in a country where the water was often tainted. Large quantities were needed). Everybody is ready for a break. From a religious point of view, the people are commemorating the forty years wandering in the wilderness under the guidance of Moses. The 'tabernacles' are the tents in which their forefathers had lived at that time. The celebrations would go on far into the night, with everywhere the people singing and dancing and blowing trumpets. But the Jews also revelled in *good* music. The Levite choir had been rehearsing Psalm 120 to 134, accompanied by a variety of instruments, in the haunting rhythm of the Hebrew verse. Every evening, standing successively on the fifteen steps leading up to the Court of the Men, they would perform them one after the other, to rapturous applause.

Each day a priest followed by a great crowd would descend the steps leading to the Pool of Siloam. He would fill a golden pitcher with water, and carry it slowly up into the temple, emptying the contents below the altar. This was to remind the people of the way in which Moses had struck a rock in the wilderness, and pure water had gushed forth.

Near the temple, two golden pillars would have been erected, each seventy-five feet high. At the top of each of them there was a container with one hundred and twenty pints of oil, and four burners. Using cast-off priests' vestments as wicks, these were lit at dusk. Since Jerusalem stood four thousand feet above the Jordan valley and the Dead Sea, the flames would have been visible for miles around. This was to remind the people of the pillar of fire which led the Children of Israel by night out of Egypt.

Now this particular Festival (mentioned in St. John's Gospel, Chapter 7) attracted a special visitor. Jesus of Nazareth slipped in quietly. According to the King James Bible there was a significant incident when early one morning He was debating in the Temple with learned men. A married woman was spotted trying to slip unobserved away from her illicit lover's home. Taking her by the arms they brought her to where Jesus and the others were talking. According to ancient law she should be stoned to death. But Jesus reminded those around Him that she was the victim of an enormously powerful instinct. It was the sort of thing that could happen in any community at any time. And marriage does sometimes turn sour. Inwardly in the broadest sense no normal person is guiltless of sexual offence. "Let him who is without sin throw the first stone," He said. Nobody could! "Sin no more," He told her.

A few years ago in Britain a young mother, Ruth Ellis, was executed for a crime of passion (her little boy, deeply affected, later took his own life). Rightly, most Britons now consider the punishment to have been barbaric. As I write there is much controversy about those unfortunate ones who are born with unnatural sexual urges that normal people find repulsive. Jesus would condemn such if they succumb to temptation, but with gentleness.

Later, Jesus watched the procession with the water. He said: "If any man thirst, let him come unto Me and drink." He watched the lighting of the flames, and He said: "I am the Light of the world. He that followeth Me shall not walk in darkness but shall have the light of life." There is a profound and very wonderful truth embedded in these words.

The Jews had a tremendous sense of God's relationship with His own chosen people. Here they were remembering how after an intense struggle they had escaped from the Egyptians. God led them towards the east with His miraculous pillar of flame. Just as they thought they had succeeded, the Egyptians decided to go after them and the pillar led them into a situation from which any possible escape was barred by the waters of the Red Sea. God saved them by sending a wind which divided the waters for them and when it subsided engulfed the Egyptian host. Later, in the wilderness, they were again faced with trouble. They could find no water to drink. God saved them by showing them how to make undrinkable contaminated water fit to drink, and again later Moses had produced his miraculous stream of water by striking a rock. God had looked after His own people. But Jesus was the light of the whole world, not just the tribe of Israel, and He would quench the thirst of any single individual man who came unto Him. He was not just concerned with a single race as such but with people *of all races* and with people *as individuals*.

Have we ever found ourselves in any situation to which in human terms there seems to be no possible answer? God is there to see us through, perhaps with answers which may surprise us. I know that to be true.

12. THE REAL WORLD

And so we come to the teaching of Jesus, and how it applies to human lives.

I used to work in the Customs in London Docks. In those days, just after the Second World War, London was the largest port in the world and how things have changed! I was the Senior Officer on just one single quay. Vast quantities of goods of every conceivable kind from all over the world came across my domain. A million cases of tea in a year, a cargo of zoo animals, a gold-mine, you name it, we had it! There was the endless stream of dockers pushing the goods into the sheds, crown-locked when not working, where they would be cleared of Customs and sent on their way. There were the shipping offices, the stevedoring companies, the Port Authority workers and the docks police. There were the lightermen whose craft took the goods to private quays. But it was a dirty, man's world. And pilfering and other forms of petty corruption were rife. Farsighted people could see the writing on the wall. Merchants wanted better treatment. The transhipment trade was slipping away to Rotterdam. Containerisation, with its greater security, was on its way. Today, it is all virtually a thing of the past.

My office was an unprepossessing corrugated iron building in the middle of it all. There were sheds on either side. It was a few feet from a Lascar lavatory. Behind it there was a small hut. That was where Harry Bass, the oiler, worked with his mate. They were both typical cockneys. But there was a difference in atmosphere. Here there was no pilfering, no bad language. The two men did an honest job.

I used to have a chat with Harry occasionally. One day he said to me: "Did you know that I've written a book?"

"I don't believe it," I said.

"Well," he said, "I'll bring you a copy tomorrow."

And he did. Harry's book was an attractive paperback, with the title *Bass of Grays* on the front. It was illustrated. I read it. Here was the story of a most appalling man. He had been a drunken lout. Any piece of thieving or mischief, and Harry had been the automatic suspect. He had been a gambler. He had woken up one morning sitting in the sink. Another time he had eaten a rabbit, innards and all. He would sing and swear in the streets in the early hours of the morning, waking everybody up. Somehow or other he acquired a wife, and they had a little girl. They both had a dreadful time. One Sunday Harry came in, rolling drunk from the pub as usual. He gave his dinner to the cat. Then he dozed off. The child made a noise. Harry in a ghastly rage lunged towards her. The mother got herself between them, and grabbed the nearest weapon, which happened to be a knife from the table. Harry, bleeding from a cut arm, went out into the street, muttering terrible oaths. Then he felt sorry for himself.

He had not gone far, when he heard cheerful singing. It was coming from the local Salvation Army Citadel. He staggered in. Those good Christian people got him to the Penitent Bench. There were no compromises, no half measures, about their requirements. There was to be no more drinking, no more gambling. Harry became a completely changed man. His home and family life became a delight. It was his Damascus Road. He became an evangelist. I have lost the book, and it is now out of print. But I shall never forget it!

And so to two similar stories. The lady running a Bible Class was delighted when one day a new boy turned up. But after the class the young people told her about the boy. He was a notorious vandal, always in trouble over something. But it was because his father was a drunkard; there was no love in his home. His decision to join the class was an act of desperation. What was she to do? The next week the young pupils were not surprised when she began to talk about how, when we are in trouble, we say our prayers. This to them was familiar ground. But of course the new boy had never heard of such a thing. He came for three weeks, then disappeared. The pupils told the teacher why. His drunken father had told him that if he went near the church again he would get the thrashing of his life. Today that boy is a habitual criminal. A failure on the teacher's part, yes, but a noble one!

The second story also concerns a parish church and its youth work. It concerns a problem family again, but this time it was the mother who was in despair. The child concerned had stolen the property of a poor old man. The church workers did not accuse him; that would have provoked an instant denial. They said to him: "You know old Mr . . . Well, we do odd jobs for him. Why not offer to cut his grass?" Old Mr . . . was the man whom he had robbed. Whether that approach worked I do not know. But it is not only the Salvation Army that has to deal with problems of this sort.

I recount these stories because of what the Gospels tell me. Over and over again we read of how Jesus consorted, not with 'respectable' people, but with sinners. He said: "They that are whole need not a physician, but they that are sick" (Luke 5.31). The rich publican

Zacchaeus, contemptuously ignored by most, was received kindly by Jesus, and repented (Luke 19:1/9). When Mary Magdalene burst in on the Pharisee's feast and anointed the feet of Jesus, the host protested. His guest should have known what sort of woman this was! Jesus rebuked him; her sins, which were many, were forgiven. "To whom little is forgiven, the same loveth little" (Luke 7:36/48). And we must take the message, mustn't we. Do not judge people by what they are like, but look deeper. Why are they as they are? And be charitable, be constructive, be helpful!

In this respect, in a slightly different sense, we sometimes come upon people who are aggressive, overbearing and rude to us. Often, they are like that because they are unsure of themselves, or because of troubles and worries in the background about which we know nothing.

Once, I discovered after meeting such a person that he had twice attempted suicide. Another was Managing Director of a Company about to be taken over by the Receivers. Another had a severe heart condition. Thank heavens in each case I swallowed my pride and exercised restraint! In the last case, in particular, the man could have died at my feet! One sometimes encounters people who are unpopular because of their boastfulness . . . Don't reject them; try a little genuine praise. It could work wonders. It may be what they desperately need! By way of analogy, a skilled driver, when his car skids, steers *towards* the skid; people are the same. Jesus always knew when to encourage, when to challenge, when to condemn, and self never entered into it . . .

13. AN ALLEGORY

I am going to give you something to think about . . . but first, a piece of fiction. Then we shall come to the thought-provoking phrase that Jesus used.

The other day I found myself reading a most fascinating children's story. It was about a farm, with a variety of livestock. The farmer was mercenary and brutal towards his animals, so much so that one day they rose up in rebellion. They drove him from his farmhouse, and set up a committee to run the farm in a more enlightened manner. For example, in the future old horses were to be provided with pasturage instead of being sent to the knacker's yard.

But gradually a change seemed to take place. The pigs dominated the committee, eventually occupying the farmhouse and learning to walk on their two back paws like men. It became apparent that the trusty old horses were being sent to the knacker's yard as before, although there was a clumsy attempt to conceal the fact. Eventually, the committee of pigs became every bit as brutal as the farmer had been . . .

Of course, this was no children's story! It was George Orwell's *Animal Farm*, an allegory based on Stalin's Russia. He was making a political point. Such is the influence of George Orwell's writings that some of his expressions have entered into everyday language. For example, if a man is referred to as 'Big Brother' it means he is overbearing and dictatorial. The words refer to a character in another of Orwell's books, *1984*.

Now I am not concerned with Orwell's political points, but his use of allegory. You see, Jesus was using an expression of this sort when He spoke of 'the sign of Jonah' (Matt. 12:39-41, repeated in Luke 11:29-32, and Matt. 16:4). Clearly this expression would have been perfectly well understood by the Pharisees who had asked Him for a sign, just as 'Big Brother' would be to us. No explanation was needed.

Jonah, like Big Brother, was a most unpleasant character. He was a prophet of the privileged chosen people of God. God told him to go and preach to the less fortunate people who lived in Nineveh. He had no desire to do any such thing, so he ran away to get away from God. His destination was Tarshish, to them the end of the earth. But God intercepted him. He was swallowed by a great fish and spewed out of its mouth. He was brought back, and God repeated his instruction. This time he had to obey. But the people of Nineveh repented. This was the last thing Jonah wanted; he wanted at least to see them punished. So he went off and sulked. Like Jonah, the Pharisees, smug and self-righteous as they were, had no wish whatsoever to share their position of privilege with other races. They understood all right, and it was to be their undoing (in the first of the two references, Jesus points out that the people of Nineveh *did* actually respond to Jonah's message, just as *they* must respond to *Him*! He was after all greater than Jonah! To men like that it must have seemed incredible that He should actually lump them together with the evil Ninevites, people like the monstrous Sennacherib of earlier times).

What about us? Are we, in our churches, perhaps sometimes like these Pharisees? Are we introspective, and unconcerned about the world outside? I am afraid that all too often we are.

I used to live in the area of the docks where the Christian churches had very little influence. In pre-war days, dock workers were treated like animals. They were herded together in 'pounds' where a few would be selected for a day's casual work. It was known for them to sell their wives' virtue in order to get chosen. It was dreadful and inhuman. All too often the churches remained aloof. They just did not want to know! They were 'middle-class' and self-contained. After the war, when the dockers had become relatively affluent and had secured regularity of employment, naturally they saw the churches as being completely irrelevant. And many a hard-working clergyman or minister has struggled hopelessly with his empty church on a vast housing estate, perhaps never even understanding why the response was so poor!

There is another way in which we can learn from the sign of Jonah. In many countries there is an extreme nationalistic element, and frequently such people liken their own supposedly superior and more virtuous countrymen to the Chosen People of God. It crops up in many places and in a variety of ways. They forget the real story of the children of Israel. The New Testament tends to depict them as being self-righteous, smug, spiritually proud and introspective; some of them actually engineered the death of the Son of God. In fact they demonstrated, not that they were more wicked, but that they were just as bad as everybody else. The story of Jonah is a warning against such attitudes.

I ask again, in these, modern, contexts . . . are we equally guilty? Is the only sign for us the sign of Jonah?

The Book of Jonah was written in the fourth century BC. Jonah was a real man, who had lived about five hundred years previously. Nineveh, destroyed in 612 BC, was in present-day northern Iraq. Tarshish was in either Spain or North Africa. The 'great fish' which 'swallowed Jonah' was Babylon, where the Jews had been exiled in the sixth century BC.

14. DEMOS

Again, concerning Jesus, I want to offer you some food for thought. This time it arises from the actual historical background to the life of Jesus.

In the first few verses of Chapter 13 of Luke's Gospel we read about 'Galileeans whose blood Pilate had mixed with their sacrifices' and about 'those eighteen upon whom the tower in Siloam fell, and slew them'. Nothing is known of the events referred to, and Jesus seems to brush them aside. But obviously the reference was to some form of demonstration or civil commotion, in which violence had occurred. The reference to Siloam suggests that the second reference might have had something to do with the water supply. It all looks like the sort of thing that could just as well happen today, with of course the bonus of television coverage.

As we have seen, our four Gospels were written long after the event. There was also a Jewish historian called Josephus, who wrote about the same area at something like the same time. But he tells some very different tales!

He tells us that at about the time of Jesus, Pontius Pilate decided to move his army from Cesarea to Jerusalem for their winter quarters. They would naturally bring their emblems with them. They came in by night, with Caesar's effigies. The Jews were outraged. Large numbers of them trooped off to Cesarea, and camped down in the central square. After six days Pilate became exasperated by their continued presence. When once again they asked for the removal of the offensive images, he gave a prearranged signal, and they were surrounded by soldiers. He told them that unless they went home immediately the soldiers would kill them. They threw themselves on the ground. They bared their necks, saying they would willingly die for their cause. Pilate relented; the images were removed.

Then Pontius Pilate found himself in trouble over water. He built an aqueduct, fifteen miles long, to bring a supply to Jerusalem, a fine feat of engineering. But he used Temple money. Tens of thousands of Jews demonstrated. Pilate brought in soldiers, disguised and carrying concealed daggers. When the crowd abused him, he gave the signal. The soldiers threw aside their cloaks and ran amok. Many Jews were killed, including some who were merely peaceful spectators.

His next short paragraph deals with "Jesus Christ". Josephus concludes by saying that the "tribe of Christians, so named after him, are not extinct to this day"! Clearly in the context of the Roman Empire they were not very numerous!

Josephus also tells us how a few years previously the Romans had sent a punitive expedition to Galilee. Sepphoris, the capital city, which was not far from Nazareth, had been destroyed by fire. After a complex series of events, two thousand young Jews had been crucified. It must have been horrible to behold! Not surprisingly, an extremist group, rather like the Provisional IRA, known as the Zealots, responded with great violence. Jesus, in Nazareth, was born and brought up against this dreadful background of events.

But Jesus, clearly, was quite unwilling to concern Himself with immediate political issues. He refused utterly to identify Himself with the particular injustices suffered by His own people, dreadful though they were. He saw mankind for what it was. He knew that there would be violent clashes of interest in every place and in every generation. He understood evil (such as the modern 'Holocaust') and it did not surprise Him. But it is difficult to imagine Him joining in with a modern 'demo', and waving banners whenever the television cameras happened to be around. His message to us all was deeper, richer, more fundamental. Everybody needs Him, regardless of race, throughout all generations. But He was no sentimentalist, as modern Christians sometimes are. By way of demonstration He had, among His closest friends, both Simon the Zealot and Matthew the Tax-gatherer (and traitor to his own persecuted race); in normal circumstances these two would have been at one another's throats. Perhaps that speaks louder than words! And what an extraordinary person Jesus must have been!

Think about all this, and form your own conclusions. For me it has led up to some interesting discussions at the door. Young University students were very much in favour of demos, whereas a retired Public School headmaster thought otherwise; it seems partly to be a matter of age and background!

15. A SIMPLE TRUTH

Sometimes the thoughts and words of Jesus are transparently simple and obviously true. Yet repeatedly as human beings we ignore them and do the opposite.

In this instance I have to start off in the Old Testament, and, curiously, the particular words of Jesus which I shall quote are not to be found anywhere in the Gospels. In fact, they were nearly lost altogether!

The somewhat obscure Book of Ecclesiastes contains the writings of several people, but the principal contributor is a man who calls himself Koheleth, the Preacher. I can only believe that his words were included in the Canon of Scripture as an example of how not to behave. He was a man of considerable wealth, and he wanted above all to be happy. First of all he sought knowledge and learning. It was 'madness and folly', 'vexation of spirit', for 'in much wisdom is much grief' (Eccles. 1:17-18). Then he tried to buy happiness with mirth and pleasure (Eccles. 2). He drank wine, he built great works, he built houses, he planted vineyards. He created gardens and orchards, and grew all kinds of fruit trees. He dug ponds. He employed servants, and acquired possessions of cattle and silver and gold. He engaged singers and musicians. And, he adds, 'whatsoever mine eyes desired I kept not from them.' But it was all 'vanity and vexation of spirit'. He was a miserable, unhappy man. Happiness cannot be bought!

So we turn to the New Testament, to the story of Paul's missionary journeys in the Acts of the Apostles.

The Jews in Jerusalem never forgave Paul for turning against them after his experience on the Damascus Road. For twenty years or so he seems to have kept away, except for a secret visit mentioned in Galatians 1:18. Then, although friends begged him to have second thoughts, he decided to return. It was a disastrous decision, leading up to imprisonment (Acts 21 onwards).

On the way his ship called at the little port of Miletus, which was about twenty miles south of Ephesus, where he had so many friends. A group of them came across to meet him for what they all clearly believed would be the last time. It was a sorrowful, emotional occasion. In his final words to them, as recorded in Acts 20:35, Paul quoted words of Jesus that occur nowhere else in Scripture: "It is more blessed to give than to receive."

The original Greek means: "It makes a person happier to give than to receive." It is such an obvious thought. Generous people are invariably happy people. The more one looks for happiness for oneself, the less likely one is to find it, but the more one seeks the happiness of others, the more likely one is to find it for oneself. A person who spends his money on providing a party for poor children at Christmas time will be far, far happier than the person who spends his money on an extravagant meal for himself. Yet so often we behave like Koheleth the Preacher and ignore the truth.

THIRD EXCURSION. ACROSS THE WATER

Preacher looks at the incomprehensible reality of eternal life.

16. HAZY VISION

I well remember the evening when my mother died. I was just home from work. I immediately got into my car, arriving at a relative's house two hundred and fifty miles away in the early hours. I dossed down; and then a surprising thing happened. I became conscious of my mother's presence. I was sure she was there in the room with me. Of course people will say it was just imagination. I can prove nothing. She stayed for about five minutes, then she was there no longer. The funeral itself was a joyful occasion, and the lovely flowers were kept for a Church Festival on the Sunday.

I told this story from the pulpit, and a worshipper wrote to the local Press. He described how, when he was small, his father had been killed in a tragic railway accident. His mother had been left, very poor, with two small children to bring up. And one day his father had come back. He spoke comforting words to his widow. She found the strength and the courage that she needed. Again this cannot be proved; sceptics would call it a matter of vivid imagination. But I believe it. Indeed I know quite well that the inexplicable does happen.

In a different sense guilt invariably forms a part of bereavement. We wish that we had acted differently towards our loved ones. We remember how we have hurt them. It is, we believe, too late now. We cannot tell them how sorry we are. I believe (and I find it a comforting thought) that those who were near to us in life are still much closer than we imagine. They *do* understand. I hope I am right.

Again in a different sense I think we all sometimes experience events which cannot be explained rationally. During the war on one occasion I was on the bridge of my ship. It was a pitch black, stormy night. I suddenly spotted, seemingly inches from the bows, a floating mine. I yelled: "Hard A'Port!", and then, to clear the stern, "Hard A'Starboard." The First Lieutenant was sleeping in his cabin at the after end of the ship, on the waterline. As the mine drifted past a few feet from his head, he woke in a cold sweat. Why?

Again, a rating on his way to join HMS *Hood* told those around him that he was going to be killed. He was right, but how did he know? A woman I know had a sixth sense that told her that an empty house was being vandalised. They went, and she was right. I once had a premonition myself, just before a serious accident. I remember, again, for no apparent reason, I felt I must visit my grandfather. He died, quite unexpectedly, three days later. None of this is scientific proof of anything. But it cannot easily be explained away.

Again, I remember when we heard that a much-loved relative of my wife's was desperately ill. I made a long journey by car, arriving at the hospital where she was at about midday. I went into the ward, and there she was. She had tubes in her throat. She was unable either to eat naturally or to speak. Around her were friends. She was writing her responses to what they said on pieces of paper. There was no sadness, just this flurry of activity which intensified as I greeted her. Do you know what she was doing? She was writing: "Poor David must be tired after his long journey. Can you arrange a meal for him?" There was no thought of self, just of me! I went off, had the meal, and returned. I stayed as long as I could, then she wrote her final message to me: "I'm not afraid if it has to come, David. It is just a slipping from one world to the next to be with the Lord and with all the dear ones gone before." True Christians know perfectly well that there is an eternity beyond the grave. It is indeed the martyr's secret that he knows that he is indestructible.

I remember another Christian friend. His lovely wife had gone out on her bicycle, and, out of the blue, she had been killed in an accident. His faith had been sorely tried. The following Sunday he managed to drag himself to the chapel he attended. The Minister's "Children's Address" was clearly intended for the very young. It was concerned with an imaginary discussion between the fruits and vegetables in a greengrocer's shop. The exotic fruits were all proclaiming their beauty and virtue, when the humble, ugly potato chipped in: "I may not be very beautiful, but I provide a solid, complete diet, and if you bury me more of my sort appear the following year." This was supposed to represent "Resurrection". Yet, absurd though it may seem, the story spoke to my bereaved friend. His wife was alive! Eternity is real!

Again, let me tell you about a boy I had in my Bible Class. I was concentrating my attention at that time on the younger secondary school age group, the eleven to fourteens. He was typical, fond of 'pop', and he played the guitar. I remember I tended to be a little off-hand with him, not really sharing his tastes. He was small for his age, and had been set on by a crowd of bullies in his younger days who had bounced on his chest. Tragically, he died suddenly of a rare lung complaint. There was a wreath at his funeral, made up in the shape of a guitar. BBC television had made a recording of his group in action, and this was transmitted after his death. So terribly, terribly sad, but for me, if only, if only, I had been more attentive! I comfort myself with the belief that perhaps somehow or other he knows how I feel.

Albert Einstein, a man of truly gigantic intellectual capacity and unique understanding of the universe, described his religious feeling as one of "rapturous amazement at the harmony of the natural law, which reveals an Intelligence of such superiority that, compared with it, all the systematic thinking of human beings is an utterly insignificant reflection". We are part of something bigger than ourselves which nobody can comprehend. Isaac Watts the hymn writer was also intellectually brilliant. He became one of the most distinguished astronomers of his day. In several of his hymns he mentions the stars with a similar sense of 'rapturous amazement'.

Scripturally, the idea expressed by Jesus at the Last Supper, of Christians joining Him for eternity in the "many mansions", would have been as much of a surprise as the Resurrection itself. On the Sabbath day the apostles would have sung psalms like the 88th. This expressed the feelings of a leper. The writer had been separated from home and neighbours. His companions in the colony were other lepers like himself, dying off one by one as their vital organs were affected. They had no hope. To them the dead just disappeared into Sheol, a place for dead bodies under the surface of a flat world. Or perhaps they might have sung the 91st, which assumed that this life of ours has to be complete in itself, with rewards for the virtuous and punishment for the wicked. But there is in pre-New Testament scripture just a glimmering of understanding in the Apocryphal Book of Wisdom, which dates from around the time of Christ (Ch. 3:1-9), words which promise eternal life for the righteous, and which incorporate the Catholic doctrine of purgatory, 'after a little chastisement they will receive great blessings'.

17. ONE MAN'S VISION

One could write a lot about Isaac Watts and the superb heritage of hymns he has left for our enjoyment and inspiration. But I should like to take just one aspect of his life, his physical self. I should like to demonstrate how this affected his thinking and his writing.

Watts had an awful life. Born in 1674, his home was within the ancient walls of Southampton. His father was in prison for practising his non-conformist faith. Southampton's walls were tall and thick (they are lovingly preserved by today's City Council). It was also protected by moats on two sides and by the sea on the other two sides. Additionally, there was a castle. In the late seventeenth century all this protection had become totally unnecessary. But this was the town which the inhabitants had inherited. They were nearly all still crammed together within an enclosed area of a tenth of a square mile. There were shops and markets, six Parish Churches, a school, as well as the people's homes. There were no proper drains or sanitation, and of course no refrigeration. The stench, the flies, the overcrowding, the unhealthy atmosphere, must have been appalling. Not surprisingly, every so often the plague would strike. The rich would escape to the country, the poor would die by the hundred. Today we talk a lot about pollution; I don't think we have the remotest idea what it used to be like!

Isaac Watts lived in the middle of all this, in a narrow, crowded road called French Street. When he was four he went to the Grammar School a few hundred yards away. And he was brilliant! But right from the start his health seems to have been impaired. He grew up small, stunted, an incredibly ugly and insignificant little man, his health a constant burden. In manhood he could not endure any sort of strain. He eventually became Minister of a chapel in the City of London, an appointment he had been reluctant to accept. Perpetual illness eventually forced him to give up his ministry in his mid-thirties. He was forced to take to his bed, and he never resumed his work. The wealthy Lord Mayor took him in hand, gave him a home, a study, and the cosseting he needed. To add to his misfortunes, throughout his early life he was dogged by religious persecution, and, for all his brilliance, both Oxford and Cambridge

Universities were barred to him. His was not a happy life!

But from his home in French Street Watts had only to walk a short distance to go out of town. Along the road he would have passed the fish market; the mind boggles at the probable stench. Then he would have passed St. Michael's Church, turned right, through the West Gate, and he was on the beach. In front to the left, he would have seen a short wharf. There would have been a number of sailing ships at anchor off the coast. A century or so previously, one of them might have been the *Mayflower*. Watts in later life had many contacts with the descendants of those who sailed in her. They had been Independents, as he was. They had suffered persecution for their faith, as he had. Now they had much in common. They corresponded, and Watts the genius became to them a great source of inspiration.

The few feet of stony beach between the walls and the water would have been polluted like everywhere else. But on a sunny day, looking beyond all this, about a mile away, Watts would have seen the fields and the trees of the New Forest, as superbly beautiful then as they are today. And he saw it through spiritual eyes: this was an illustration of his own life story. His was a stunted body living in foul surroundings. But beyond this life his misery would be transformed into something indescribably wonderful. "There is a land of pure delight," he wrote, "Where saints immortal reign." In superb poetry, he went on to describe how death, like a narrow sea, divides this heavenly land from ours, and how timorous mortals start and shrink to cross the narrow seas.

This, I believe, is one of the most beautiful hymns ever written, and the tune 'Beulah' fits it like a glove. Yet it is rarely sung. Could it be that we 'timorous mortals' dislike talking about death, even those of us who are Christians?

We should, in my view, certainly be singing this hymn on Remembrance Sunday, when we are thinking of those who died sadly and prematurely. But we never do. Instead, we sing another Watts hymn, "O God our Help in Ages Past", which speaks of eternity in a grander, broader way. After the words "We *will* remember them" we cast our minds back through forty or fifty years and picture to ourselves those friends and relatives who died; then we sing the hymn, which includes the words: "Time like an ever rolling stream bears all its sons away". And then: "They fly *forgotten* as a dream dies at the opening day" – not really the sort of thought we need to have when we are trying to remember! I would prefer the other hymn.

FOURTH EXCURSION. THE CHILDREN'S PLAYGROUND

Preacher looks at children's addresses. His words are simple, but his stories as such would be equally suitable for adults. For brevity's sake he has, here and there, used words which might not be understood by young children. Frequently, he would use visual aids as the basis of such talks. Favourites in this respect are a miniature Bible with magnifying glass, which he conceals in a matchbox. He hides the matchbox in a hollowed-out book, and gets a child to play the 'Customs Officer' in a country in which the Bible is prohibited. He also has an enormous banner which unwinds to reveal the name "Llanfairpwllgwyngyllgogerychwyrndrobwll-llantysiliogogogoch"! The name links "St. Mary's Church" (Llanfair) with a tiny church on an island in the middle of the Menai Strait called "St. Tysilio's" where services are held during the summer. It is a sentence, not a word. The "gogo goch" or "red cave" at the end is part of the construction of Telford's famous 'Menai Suspension Bridge'.

18. SEA STORIES

Now, children, do you think that I am completely bonkers (answer, predictably, "Yes". Attention now guaranteed!)? Well, now, listen . . . When I was a Naval Officer during the war I recall that we were once operating off the coast of Newfoundland. I was on the bridge of my ship. We were travelling at full speed, about eighteen knots, in smooth seas and deep water, Nothing remarkable about that, you would say. But just listen . . .

You see, we were in thick, thick fog. I could barely see the men on the sides of the bridge, or the funnel behind me. I certainly could not see the man in the bows. Yet I was quite happy.

We had Radar. In a caboose behind me a man was watching a screen that looked like a television screen. We were in the centre. He could see the coastline on the starboard side. He could see any other ships or obstructions that might be around us. He could plot us on the chart. We were perfectly safe.

Life is like that. We cannot see where we are going, especially if we are young. I imagine you young people in front of me as you will be in twenty or thirty years' time. Amazing, exciting, but totally unpredictable things lie ahead of you. But we need the Radar, the unseen guide that is there to guide us and to protect us, if we are to make the most of ourselves. We call it Christianity. We must keep it in good order, and observe what it tells us. As Paul says: "We walk by faith, not by sight" (2 Cor. 5:7).

You boys and girls have life in front of you, and you haven't the remotest idea what you will be doing in twenty years' time. But it will be wonderful and surprising. Do let God guide you!

Again, there is the story of the Eddystone lighthouse. Barely visible rocks near the busy sea lanes outside Plymouth caused numerous tragedies, so they decided to mark them with a light. The first lighthouse was an extraordinary affair, made of wood, with flags and a sort of pagoda-like roof. It blew over in its first winter. They tried again, with a lighthouse built smooth and round like an oak. But after a few years it caught fire. So they had another go. The third was made of stone, with a smooth round shape. But they found after a few years that it was founded on a wobbly rock. They took it down and re-erected it on Plymouth Hoe. The fourth, firmly based on solid rock, is there today (here, I produce a 1964 penny, which has an image of the third Eddystone Lighthouse behind the figure of Britannia).

A young person growing up is like this. We 'sow our wild oats', as they say. We make mistakes, and we correct them, as the lighthouse builders did. We do silly things. But eventually if the will is there we make it, becoming 'lights set upon a hilltop' and guides to others – in fact, just like a lighthouse!

19. LAMPS

The other day I took my grandchildren to the caves at Llanelwy. Have you ever been there? They are very old. Human remains have been found going back tens of thousands of years.

We found them all right. But the moment we got inside we were in trouble. You see, it was pitch dark; and the rocky floor was not at all smooth. We found ourselves tripping up and falling over.

But we had thought of that. We had brought oil-lanterns, which we lit. Then, if we held them near our feet, we could see where we were treading, and we could go quite a distance into the caves (here I show them a lantern).

The Bible is like that. It says in one of the psalms that God's Word is a lamp unto our feet and a light unto our paths. Learn to read it as you grow up; more and more you will find out how true that is!

But I remember once a long time ago I found a different cave. I was in Campbeltown in Scotland. I walked across a causeway to the tiny island of Davaar, then along the rocky beach to a cave in the cliff. This cave has a shaft of light at the far end, and somebody has painted on the flat rock there a picture of Jesus. Everything around me was so beautiful, and here I was in the dark cave suddenly discovering the Light of Life!

And now again I am going to tell you another story that will make you think that I am bonkers!

Sometimes I go into a padded room all by myself. It has double doors and thick windows. Very little sound gets in from outside. I sit down. And I talk!

There is a red light glowing. Around me are all sorts of gadgets, turntables to play records, and so on. In front of me there is a microphone – and that gives the game away! You guessed, didn't you? I am broadcasting, talking to lots of people whom I cannot see.

It is something like what we all do every day. You say your prayers, don't you? You can't see God. But He is there, in a wonderful sort of way. The older you get the more you will understand, as we grown-ups understand. But say your prayers, and keep on doing it always. We need our prayers to guide us, as well as the Bible.

20. MICE

You know, one of my jobs is to show people around Bangor Cathedral. It is the oldest Cathedral in England and Wales, because Saint Deiniol, the man who first built a church there, came in 524 AD, a very, very long time ago. He built a tiny wooden church, with a fence round it. The word he used for the wooden fence was 'bangor', which means 'wattle bark'. That is why the city, which was built later around the church, was called "Bangor". Because the cathedral is so interesting, people come from all over the world to see it. I talk to them.

But when I see small children coming in with their parents, they often look bored. So for a start I show them the dog-tongs. If dogs come in and bark, we can catch them round their necks, and push them outside again. Then I ask them: "Do you like mice, because there are mice here!"

The boys say: "I don't mind", but the girls often say: "No!" Then I explain. Our mice are not live mice. You see, there was a very clever woodcarver who came from Yorkshire, and he made a lot of the beautiful carvings you can see here, as well as what he did in lots of other places. But whenever he made anything, he always ended up by carving on it a little mouse (I tell them to come and look at the one on the font). Then I tell them that there are three more; can they try and find them? And they go and look.

But why did the carver always put mice on what he did? I'll tell you; when he was a young man, he was very poor. But when he became older, and famous, he became quite rich. But he always wanted to remember that once he had been poor, just like a 'church-mouse', but that God had given him clever hands to make him rich. It was his way of saying thank you to God.

Do you say thank you to God for things, like your home and your mothers and fathers and your food and the games you play and your toys . . . ? So many things, aren't there! You must!

21. AN AIR STORY

For young people, not children . . .

Many years ago, when I was running a Bible Class, I had a boy in my group who was rightly very proud indeed of his father. His father was a Senior Pilot with the British Overseas Airways Corporation, and he had been specially selected for a new job.

At that time passenger aircraft were driven by propellors and reciprocating engines. They were noisy, rattly, uncomfortable and slow. But then the jets arrived, in the form of the De Havilland *Comet*. The boy's father was to fly one of these new wonder planes, so steady and so smooth that one could drink a cup of tea without spilling a drop, while flying at a great height and at an enormous speed.

But the Comets were faulty. First one, then another, exploded in mid-air. The third to go was the one piloted by the boy's father – it happened over shallow waters off the Italian coast. This time all the planes were grounded. They recovered the bits of wreckage and discovered where the defect lay. It was an enormous job.

But the boy's father was safe; you see, he had been on holiday when it had happened!

The father was a devout Christian, and he took this to be a sign. He gave up flying, except to fly as a passenger to central Africa. There he became the humblest of missionaries, looking after a bookroom in the heart of the bush. He was poor, but he was doing what God wanted him to do. That is how God sometimes speaks to us.

FIFTH EXCURSION. THE NEW SUBURB

Preacher looks beyond the Gospels to the rest of the New Testament.

22. INDIVIDUAL CHALLENGE

Jesus was no longer physically present in the early Church, but He lived on in the Spirit. His followers through all generations were to be His physical presence in the world which God had made. His voice, His arms, His legs, His eyes.

One day Jesus had met a rich young man, and told him that he should give up all he possessed (Luke 18:18-27). But the challenge was too much for him; he just could not give up his great wealth in order to follow Jesus. He went away, sorrowful. Jesus said: "The things which are impossible with men are possible with God."

His name was Joseph. How do I know? Well, after completing his Gospel, Luke went on to write "The Acts of the Apostles". He described with gusto the early Christian Church (Acts 4:32-37). Those were wonderful times. The believers were united in body and soul, with everything held in common. Those who had property sold it, giving the money for distribution to those in need. Then Luke described one particular man, Joseph, a Levite and a native of Cyprus, who sold his estate. It was, almost certainly, a reference to the rich young man, who had indeed found that with God's help he could meet the challenge. Anybody with any experience of land management will know what a perpetual tie it is! Joseph was now free. The others gave him a nickname, Barnabas, which means 'one who encourages others'.

The good times did not last. The Jewish leaders had a conscience about the death of Jesus. Deep down within themselves they must have known that they had done wrong. But they would not admit it. Instead, they persecuted the Christians. There was one arrogant, intelligent, vicious young man who brought them much distress. One day, having discovered that Christianity was spreading, the young man went off to spread the persecution. A week or two later he returned. He told a 'cock and bull' story that surely nobody would believe, about how he had encountered the living Christ outside Damascus. He said he was a changed man. Obviously, they thought, it was a blatant piece of chicanery; he wanted to find out the secrets of the Christians from inside so that he could harm them the more. They didn't believe him and didn't want him . . . except, that is, for one man. Barnabas said: "I believe him", and talked the others into taking a chance. Paul became one of them. But the Jews now saw him as a quisling. For his own safety he had to get away. He went north and across the sea to his own city of Tarsus.

Seventeen or more years now passed, about which we know little. There was apparently some contact between Paul and Barnabas (Gal. 2:1). But then glad news came the way of the believers. Three or four hundred miles north of Jerusalem, on the coast, was to be found the great city of Antioch. In size and importance it almost equalled Rome itself. Basking in the Mediterranean sunshine it was a beautiful place. There was an abundant supply of pure fresh water, and the inhabitants were perpetually bathing. It had wide streets, fine buildings, even street lighting. The news was . . . people there were prepared to embrace Christianity. They despatched Barnabas. He found that it was indeed as they had been told. Then he did something strange. Instead of working on it, he went away to Tarsus to see if he could find Paul. He found him, after all those years, brought him back, and they worked together.

After a year, talking together, they thought: "Why not go off together on an evangelising mission?" And where better than Barnabas' home territory? They went off to Cyprus on what we now call: "St. Paul's First Missionary Journey". They had a wonderful time, as they journeyed along the southern coast and then across the sea to the north . . . but for one thing. They had with them a youth, Barnabas' nephew, who evidently was not very reliable. He eventually deserted them.

After returning home, the two men began to think about going again, this time further afield. But there was a dispute between them. Barnabas wanted to give the youth another chance. Paul said no. Barnabas and Paul separated. Barnabas went off with the youth, and we lose sight of him, because "Acts" concentrates on what Paul did.

So think back! If it had not been for Barnabas, Paul would not even have been accepted into the Christian community. If it had not been for Barnabas he would not have been brought to Antioch or undertaken his missionary journeys. If it had not been for Barnabas, the unreliable youth, whose services Paul wanted to reject, would probably have given up altogether. He was in fact Mark, who later on wrote the earliest Gospel, known as "Peter's Gospel", because he was with Peter in Rome. The encourager was responsible for all that!

Why not copy Barnabas? Think . . . do you know, from among your relatives or friends, anybody who could do with a bit of encouragement? Act; there is no telling what good you might achieve.

And preachers can encourage the encouragers, can't they! What an opportunity!

23. MAN AND WIFE
In a deeper, richer sense this applies to successful marriage. Husband and wife encourage each other, build each other up. Marriage must never ever be allowed to become a competition.

During the last century General Lew Wallace was returning east from his spell as Governor of Arizona with Robert G. Ingersoll, the notorious agnostic and enemy of Christianity. As they approached the city of St. Louis they remarked on the great forest of steeples and towers which indicated the presence of churches. How pathetic, they thought! Then Ingersoll had an idea. "Why not," he said to Wallace, "write a book which will disprove once and for all this foolish superstition?"

Wallace accepted the challenge. He went home, told his wife (who was a practising Methodist) and set to work. He was thorough in his research. The project took several years. He had written the first four chapters, when he made a discovery. Jesus was as real as Socrates, Plato, Caesar; and all that was claimed for Him was true. It was Wallace's Damascus Road. One night, for the first time ever, he knelt down and prayed. Then, in the early morning, he went into his wife's room and told her. They knelt down together. "O Lew," she said, "I have prayed for this ever since you started this silly book. My prayers have been answered." They agreed then and there . . . the book would be, not what was originally intended, but a testimony to the way in which one man found the truth.

Later, in 1878, Lew Wallace accepted an appointment as Governor of New Mexico. He settled into his picturesque old Spanish residence in

Santa Fe. It was a dangerous mission. This was a violent community in which murder was commonplace, but it has acquired a certain misplaced glamour as the backdrop to innumerable Hollywood 'westerns'. Among the most notorious bandits was Billy the Kid, who boasted that he had killed twenty-one men before he was twenty-one. But at night Wallace was able to push his unpleasant responsibilities to one side and to work on what was to bring him lasting fame. It was a very long book, written in purple ink in numerous bound notebooks. At last it was ready for the publishers. With its well-known author it became the literary sensation of 1881. Wallace, his task completed, went off to become American Ambassador to Turkey.

The book is called *A Tale of the Christ*. It is imaginative fiction, unsentimental and full of dramatic incident, but it brings in, in a most moving and original way, all the main events in the life of Christ. The Jewish hero and his family end up as a Christian family during the earliest days of the Church. However, the book has another, more familiar, title, *Ben Hur*. Paradoxically, it has attracted the film makers, because of one dramatic event, ideal for filming, the famous chariot race. Otherwise, it might have been forgotten. Those who turn from film to book must find themselves uplifted by what it contains. It would never have been written but for Mrs. Wallace.

I, personally, owe an enormous debt of gratitude to my own wife (and I know that wives, equally, sometimes owe a great debt to their husbands). But no two marriages are alike. I proposed to my wife on the day she had been told by the consultant surgeon that she would have to abandon the nursing that she loved. We have had to face up together to the war nerves from which I suffered in 1946 and to her repeated long and worrying spells in hospital before and when our two children were growing up. Today we have an extended family which includes great grandchildren, a close-knit loving group of seventeen people which started with the promises we made at the altar over fifty years ago, for better, for worse, in sickness and in health. Of course there have been deep-seated tensions at times, but isn't that what life is all about? My wife is to me a treasure beyond price. At the time of writing I have just read the moving story of a Methodist Minister who at the beginning of his career became completely deaf. He has a wife who must have sustained him in all his difficulties, and two sons. There must have been tensions, but he also lives in an obviously loving and developing relationship like mine (*Seeing is Hearing*, by Will Morrey, University of Wales, Bangor).

24. PRISON

We turn now to another Christian book, perhaps, apart from the Bible, the most widely read of all, although it has never attracted the attention of Hollywood in quite the same way.

The writer of *The Pilgrim's Progress* was John Bunyan, an uneducated tinker, with a rare gift of expression. He was a Baptist, and strongly Protestant. He knew his Bible intimately. But one day he searched in vain for a favoured Text, "Look at the generations of old and see; did any ever trust in the Lord and was confounded?" To his disgust he found it in the Apocrypha (Ecclesiasticus 2:10). Only the Roman Church regarded this as scriptural; he described it as a "jewel in a swine's snout"! He preached wherever he could find an audience. But with such an outlook, in the seventeenth century, trouble was inevitable. He broke the laws which protected the Anglican form of worship. He was sent to prison for twelve years from 1660, and he served a further six-month sentence in 1675. In prison he was forced into a life of meditation and passive creativity. The twelve years produced many books and pamphlets. The six months produced the first part of *The Pilgrim's Progress*. Had he not been imprisoned, his genius would have died with him. Like the 'generations of old', he had 'trusted in the Lord' and was not 'confounded'.

So it was with Paul. In his perpetual activity he resembled Bunyan.

He was a 'live wire'. But he too spent many years in prison, in seemingly frustrating idleness. The four *Prison Epistles* which have survived include some of his greatest gifts to posterity. Many of his finest books were not written in prison as such, but in his day there was another form of enforced idleness. *We* complain if we are held up for twenty-four hours at Heathrow but travellers like Paul in New Testament times could be delayed for months on end, aboard sailing ships either held up by gales or becalmed and stationary!

However, I wonder how many of my readers have even the remotest idea what it is like to be imprisoned in the legal sense. In any part of the world in any age it would be very much the same. There is the sheer frustration of it, with the interminable boredom of one year or two years or whatever the sentence might have been. There is the crowding, the utter impossibility of finding any privacy. There are the crude basic toilet facilities. But on top of that there is the nature of the company with which one is forced to live. These are criminals, social failures, some merely pathetic, others thoroughly bad. Unnatural practices occur. Dirty speech is commonplace. Those imprisoned for their principles, prisoners of conscience, have to serve their time with the rest. John Bunyan and Paul both suffered in this way.

One day Paul's friends outside sent him a present. He wrote a 'thank you' letter which providentially has been preserved. It is an absolute gem. It is called: *The Epistle to the Philippians.* How was he coping? Well, he wrote the immortal words: "Whatsoever things are true, whatsoever things are honest, whatsoever things are just, whatsoever things are pure, whatsoever things are lovely, whatsoever things are of good report; if there be any virtue, and if there be any praise, think on (fill your mind with) these things" (Ch. 4:8). He had cocooned himself, made himself into an island of wholesome thoughts. It was such 'wholesome thoughts', Spirit guided meditation if you like, that enabled him to write as he did.

The most extraordinary aspect of this letter is the happiness expressed. Certainly he can speak of his friends outside as 'longed for' (Ch. 4:1). What an understatement that must have been; one can well imagine how much he wanted Christian companionship! But "Rejoice in the Lord," he says, "and again I say rejoice!" (Ch. 4:4). Then he goes on: "And the peace of God, which passeth all understanding, shall keep your hearts and minds through Jesus Christ" (Ch. 4:7). There he was, deep in the deepest of troubles. And he found, as so many others have found, not a sense of utter hopelessness, but a wonderful tranquillity. It was beyond his understanding, but it was there. He would have been reminded of the words of Jesus to his desperately frightened apostles in the Upper Room: "My peace I leave with you." So, he goes on, "I have learned, in whatsoever state I am, therewith to be content" (Ch. 4:11). Don't kick against misfortune! Accept it, even *enjoy* it! "Be careful for nothing," he says – don't *worry* about things! "But in everything by prayer and supplication let your requests be made known unto God" (Ch. 4:6). "I can do all things through Christ which strengtheneth me" (Ch. 4:13), he adds. In those squalid surroundings God had become very close indeed; He always is nearest to us when we need Him most. And in verse 5 Paul tells us that we must let our moderation be known unto all men. Moderation? Hardly the quality which we associate with some forms of Christianity!

Paradoxically, the evil of his imprisonment actually brought good in its wake. It gave us this superb epistle. But also, to quote: "I would ye should understand, brethren, that the things which happened unto me have fallen out rather unto the furtherance of the gospel; so that my bonds in Christ are manifest in all the palace, and in all other places; and many of the brethren in the Lord, waxing confident in my bonds, are much more bold to speak the word without fear" (Ch. 1:12-14).

I urge you to read the whole Epistle! It is short – and magnificent! In modern times, Terry Waite's incarceration reminded me of all this. He was locked away, suffering the most appalling deprivation, for five dreadful years. Just before his release he received a postcard, a picture of the imprisoned Bunyan, writing, one assumes, *The Pilgrim's Progress*. So very appropriate! But, unlike Bunyan, Terry's moderation was known to all men; the present-day Church of England, his church, at its magnificent best, is a church of moderation. He praised the Muslim faith of his captors, calling it a 'noble faith'. He was, like St. Paul, 'all things to all men' – he respected the beliefs of others. He enjoyed no physical protection; but he did wear, like St. Paul, the 'whole armour of God' – see my next chapter. He endured it all in faith, his own Christian faith.

25. LET'S GO ON

So we come to another letter that St. Paul wrote from prison. But first, some background . . .

The book we call "The Acts of the Apostles" is just about the longest book in the New Testament. But it comes to an abrupt end. In those days writing books was an incredibly clumsy business. The author would buy a scroll of papyrus, derived from the inner bark of a plant. It would have a cylindrical container. The words, frequently Greek, would be written in vertical columns about three inches wide, without punctuation. The finished article would be fragile in the extreme, and, if used a lot, would soon need replacement. There was a vast army of scribes, equipped with quill pen and ink, whose function was to copy. Against this background it is quite amazing that we have a New Testament at all, and that it is as accurate as it seems to be. My theory about "Acts" is quite simply that Luke ran out of scroll, or that he started a fresh scroll that has since disappeared.

Be that as it may, the book tells us how the great evangelist Paul at last achieved his ambition. He came to Rome, the heart of the Roman Empire, the great imperial city with perhaps a million and a half inhabitants. Then it fizzles out!

This would have happened round about 59 AD. If we look in our history books we will find that the Emperor at the time was Nero. He was a monster, comparable to Hitler. In 54 AD his mother had murdered his father. In 55 AD he consolidated his position as Emperor by murdering the rightful heir. There follows a quite appalling period of immorality and viciousness in high places. Then in 59 AD he committed a crime so vile that even he felt he must go away for a little while. The crime? He murdered his own mother! There was a mighty thunderstorm in Rome, suggesting to the superstitious that even the gods were angry. Then he returned – and found that the Senate, far from condemning what he had done, had made him a god and erected a statue in his honour. They were as bad as he was! In 61 AD Nero's soldiers invaded Anglesey and defeated the Druids in their heartland – his sphere of influence, the Roman Empire, was truly enormous (I am writing these words in Anglesey). In 64 AD we have the great fire of Rome, during which 'Nero fiddled'. He looked for somebody to blame. The peace loving, gentle, harmless Christians made a convenient scapegoat. Men, women and children were thrown to hungry animals in the arena while great crowds watched. Piso rebelled against him, and failed. Vindex also failed. But in 68 AD Galba was successful, and the tyrant killed himself with his own sword. So (until he was martyred) the great evangelist and the great monster were actually living in the same city – and Acts tells us nothing!

I attended a course at St. Deiniol's Residential Library in Hawarden, at which our tutor was an old Bishop in his eighties. St. Deiniol's contains Gladstone's superb library. There is nothing quite like it anywhere else in the world.

And what a man our tutor was! He was so lively, so much of an evangelist, that when we heard him talking about the epistles it was as if Paul himself was speaking. He told us that he was convinced that during that period when Paul was a prisoner in his own rented house in Rome, he wrote the Epistle to the Ephesians.

Certainly 'Ephesians' makes stimulating reading. In style it is unique. "We wrestle not against flesh and blood, but against principalities, against powers, against the rulers of the darkness of this world, against spiritual wickedness in high places." The cosmic powers of darkness, certainly, but was not Nero and all he stood for a human embodiment of such devilish evil? Paul looked at the soldier perpetually guarding him. He wrote about "the whole armour of God . . . loins girt about with truth . . . the breastplate of righteousness . . . shod with the preparation of the

Gospel of peace . . . the shield of faith . . . the helmet of salvation . . . praying always". Such exciting, familiar words! The Bishop thought that the 'fiery darts of the wicked' were words arising from the thunderstorm; fiery darts are fired at buildings, not soldiers.

Elsewhere in Ephesians there is a vivid call to Christian unity. We are reminded too that we do not live in our own strength. "By grace are ye saved through faith; and that not of yourselves: it is the gift of God." But to me the most remarkable passage occurs at the point where the highly articulate Paul actually finds himself lost for words! He cannot describe in adequate human terms the love of Christ. So he says "it passeth knowledge", and it has "breadth and length and depth and height". His knowledge of Euclid's geometry told him that an object with four dimensions was inconceivable. So it was with Christ's love; it was quite beyond our human conception.

More magnificent stuff from the ambassador in bonds! Again, read it in its entirety!

26. NOBLE RUIN
Shall we go to Ephesus, then?

Many tourists today do just that. Turkey is a wonderful country to visit. Ephesus was once a prosperous port on its western coastline. It is now deserted, and the harbour has silted up. But the remains of this once beautiful city are in a fine state of preservation. Visitors come by the thousand. They walk along the ancient street, with its ruined buildings on either side, temples, shopping arcades, houses, public buildings. The city had its great air-conditioned library and its facilities for sports and the arts. Outside the city stood one of the seven wonders of the world, the Temple of Diana. And there is today the great basilica built over the tomb of John the Apostle . . .

In imagination I tried to think of myself going back in time, not quite to St. Paul's time, but to about 90 or 100 AD. The city came to life. The harbour was full of ships. There were people of all nationalities walking around. There were chariots. There was bustling activity everywhere.

But this, I told my imagination, is Sunday. I should like to go to church. So, in my broken Greek, I made some inquiries. The church took some finding, because few of the inhabitants were Christians; but eventually, off the beaten track, I discovered their meeting place. I joined them.

They told me that this was an organised, well-established church. Some of them certainly remembered Paul and Peter, but the two men, sadly, had been martyred thirty or more years ago. They were part of history now. Every Sunday there was the breaking of bread. There was singing, and some preaching. There were prayers. And they had a collection of scrolls, from which they read.

The New Testament as such had not been put together at that time. One imagines that travellers, visiting such a place, might have said: "You know, you must get a copy of (shall we say) that book by so-and-so", and arrangements would have been made for a copy. Some of their scriptures might have been outside our New Testament; there might have been, for example, Clement's Epistle to the Corinthians, a popular tract which was lost until it turned up again in England in 1628!

So, I joined them, a happy group, men and women of all ages. And then it happened! A group of young men carried in an old, old man. They all looked at him, love and affection in everybody's eyes. Who could this be? They explained; he was John, yes, John the Apostle whom Jesus loved, still miraculously alive, still intellectually alert despite his feeble body. This was their precious link with the past, the one remaining link with Jesus Himself. He had looked after Mary in her cottage in the woods until she died; and here he still was. Most scholars will reject what I have written as being disproven fantasy, but I have described what the church traditionally believed until just a few years ago. The tradition continues with the belief that the leaders of the church one day said to the old man: "Look, we know you can't live for ever. We have the other Gospels; but would you, before you die, tell us your story of Jesus?" They prayed and they fasted for three days, then John started: "In the beginning was the Word . . . " And, with breaks, he continued right through to the end, when in a fit of final exasperation he said: "And there are also many other things which Jesus did, the which, if they should be written every one, I suppose that even the world itself could not contain the books that should be written."

I once attended a course at Oxford. Our Tutor was the unique and wonderful William Barclay. Few men have combined the qualities of scholarship and the common touch quite as he did. He believed that the fourth gospel was written by John the Apostle. Perhaps he was led more by his heart than by his mind. I don't know!

John's Gospel, as my readers will know, is a superb devotional book, quite different in style and content from the other three. It can be read in a straightforward way and is most rewarding. But when one looks at it more deeply one finds hidden treasure.

John does not repeat the story about the bread and the wine, but he devotes five whole precious chapters to the Last Supper. Symbolically he makes the death of Jesus coincide with the sacrifice of the Paschal Lamb, and the Last Supper becomes the supper before the Passover Feast. His Gospel contains seven 'signs', from the wedding in Cana to the resurrection appearance of Jesus to doubting Thomas.

At the wedding Jesus turns some thirty gallons of water into wine, an enormous quantity. Is John saying "How bountiful God is"; or is he saying: "This is an allegory"? In the raising of Lazarus from the dead, there is a conversation between Jesus and Martha which is clearly concerned with *spiritual* life and death: "Whosoever liveth and believeth in Me shall never die." When Lazarus emerged from the tomb, Jesus said: "Loose him and let him go." Is this an allegory too? Was the death of Lazarus a spiritual death caused by some outbreak of sinfulness on his part? We shall never know; but I do find it strange that the first mentioned phrase is used out of context in funeral services. John also tells the story of a crippled beggar who lay all day by the pool of Bethesda. Jesus healed him, but later told him to 'sin no more'. What was his 'sin'? Could it possibly be that he had been a fraud, making an easy income out of the charity of others? Again, we shall never know.

But there is no doubt about other expressions with double meanings. When Judas Iscariot left the Upper Room to betray Jesus, John writes: "And it was night." It was – but it was more than that: there was a deep spiritual darkness over the whole world. Years ago, I went one Sunday to a small Methodist church in the Cotswolds. The sparsely attended morning service was conducted by a young Local Preacher. Half-way through a man came in. He whispered to the preacher on the platform, who then said to us: "Mr. Chamberlain has just said on the wireless that we are at war with Germany." We all became quiet and sad; one woman wept openly. Night, in the sense that John uses it, had descended upon us.

When Mary, the sister of Lazarus, broke a jar of costly ointment over the feet of Jesus, wiping them with her hair, in thankfulness for the raising of her beloved brother, John says that the whole house was filled with the fragrance. It would have been; but is there not also a spiritual fragrance about a loving deed? And when Jesus spoke about being "lifted up", is there not also a clear double meaning? John deserves to be looked at closely.

Search the Gospel. There are riches to be discovered in John's writings which are far from obvious to the merely casual reader.

27. PLACE OF EXILE

Not far from Ephesus there is an island that we must visit, but it presents some difficulty. Ephesus is in Moslem Turkey; the island is in Christian Greece, the country where the language of the New Testament is still in everyday use. The tension between the two religions goes back to the Crusades and beyond. So we may not be able to make a direct journey.

The tradition is that the aged John was exiled to the island (called Patros) during a time of persecution, perhaps around 96 AD. There (again according to tradition) he wrote Revelation, the last book in the Bible. The style is quite different from that of his Gospel. But in those dangerous times his message had to be coded; he could even have confused any Roman reader by writing the original version in his own minority language, Aramaic. Our (Greek) version may be a translation. But this is unimportant.

The book is a collection of poetic visions. The writer obviously had with him an Old Testament, and much of what he wrote arises from the writings of the prophets. The mystic number seven constantly appears. A very old scholarly book tells me that Revelation contains an example of a particular style, which for preachers would be quite unsuitable, and which, anyway, I would never have noticed myself! The climax appears in the middle, with three ascending steps leading towards it and three descending steps leading from it. The apex is the Kingdom of the world becoming the Kingdom of Christ (Ch. 11:19 to 15:4). The sealed book, the seven seals and the seven trumpets lead up to it (vide Ch. 4 & 5, Ch. 6 to 8:4, and Ch. 8:5 to 11:18); and beyond it further images form a descending order, the seven golden bowls, judgment enthroned, and the New Jerusalem (Ch. 15:5 to Ch. 19:4; Ch. 19:5 to Ch. 20; and Ch. 21 to Ch. 22:5, respectively). Clearly there is a highly sophisticated subtlety about this book, not apparent to the casual reader; the author must have been a man of considerable intelligence. Although the language and ideas are completely different it reminds one of St. John's Gospel. John's Gospel contains seven signs, as I mentioned in my previous chapter. 'Revelation' does also, however, contain some truly magnificent passages and much to inspire the preacher.

What is important, however, is that some readers have treated these apocalyptic writings as if they were some sort of code predicting such matters as the end of the world. John, like other New Testament writers, saw the end as being imminent; he was wrong. It raises the whole question of scripture and its interpretation.

It is possible to prove almost anything by the selective use of biblical texts. One can justify apartheid. One can justify the sexual abuse of children. How can we protect ourselves from misinterpretation? Some would say that the Bible was put together by the Church, and therefore the Church is the ultimate authority. But the Church, through the ages, has demonstrated its human fallibility many times. So where do we stand?

Dare I suggest that once again we are forgetting the third part of the Trinity, that part of God which is within us and around us (see what I wrote about prayer earlier in this book)? The Holy Spirit tells us what is obviously good and inspiring, and what is bad. I cannot believe, for example, that blood transfusions are wrong when they make such a great contribution to human wellbeing, despite what the Bible might seem to say – any more than I can believe that healing on the Sabbath is wrong! Yet some people would 'prove' by scriptural chapter and verse that these things *are* wrong! I do not believe that Chapter 8 of the Book of Revelation is about the explosion of the Nuclear Power Station at Chernobyl, as some would have me think. I think Jesus by *His* attitude showed us clearly what *our* attitude should be. The Book of Revelation (and similar writings) can lead us up the garden path, if it is treated as a sort of coded prediction of future events. Dare I even use the word 'commonsense'? Coupled with intuition, surely the vehicle of the Holy Spirit!

I believe myself that women should be ordained if they have the calling and the ability. I believe that contraception within marriage is legitimate and desirable. And I believe that family planning should be given every sort of encouragement in countries in which over-population is a problem. My intuition, my commonsense, my personal assessment, in all humility, of what the Living Christ would say!

28. GRATEFULNESS
As another example, Christians don't need books to tell them that they should have thankful hearts. Let me demonstrate.

Historically much of the seventeenth century in England was horrible. But it did start with Shakespeare, whose plays appeared between 1588 and 1613. And in 1611 the Authorised Version of the Bible was published in all its superb beauty. It contains a strangely obscure compliment to the Bard in Psalm 46, in which the 46th word from the beginning and the 46th word from the end made up the word "Shakespeare". Shakespeare had a comprehensive knowledge of earlier editions of the Bible, including the Apocrypha. Forty-two biblical books have been identified in his plays. It affected his thinking. Numerous passages could be quoted. Just one example – the familiar phrase which begins: "The quality of mercy is not strained" is actually inspired by a phrase from Ecclesiasticus (Ch. 35:20 – "Mercy is seasonable in the time of affliction, as clouds of rain in the time of drought"). Portia was rebuking Shylock the Jew with a quotation from his own Jewish scripture, their so-called and obviously important "Church Book" ("Ecclesiasticus" in Greek).

Otherwise it was a period of the most wicked religious persecution. In 1620 the Mayflower sailed away across the Atlantic to escape from it all. The Presbyterians, the Baptists, the Anglicans, the Catholics were all at one another's throats. King James could hardly have read the Bible which he authorised; in 1612 he ordered the execution by burning of Legate and Wightman, purely because of their religious beliefs. There was a dreadful period in the 1650s when many women were murdered because of alleged 'witchcraft'. In 1645 the Archbishop of Canterbury was beheaded; the king followed in 1649. In 1645 the Prayer Book was banned. The Bishops and Deans were removed. Many Anglican priests were deprived of their livings and reduced to a state of abject poverty. And in Ireland there was the dreadful slaughter which affects us all still. One could go on.

But through all this time there was one clergyman who simply persisted with his calling. His name was Edward Reynolds. He had no time whatsoever for all this vicious intolerance. He was a generous, warm-hearted, kindly, happy Christian pastor. Born in 1599, the year in which Shakespeare's Globe Theatre was built, he saw it all. In 1661 the monarchy had been restored and a new Book of Common Prayer was needed.

They tried to make it ecumenical, but the twenty-four Anglican and Presbyterian scholars appointed to create the book soon squabbled. The Anglicans finished the job. Reynolds, Presbyterian though he had been, gladly accepted the post of Bishop of Norwich, and paid from his own pocket for necessary repairs to the Cathedral. And he made his own special contribution to posterity. He wrote the General Thanksgiving for the new book. It is, I suggest, much more than a prayer. It is a reflection of a beautiful, and tested, Christian personality. It should be introduced as such. Those interested can find a complete set of Reynolds' writings in the Norwich Cathedral Library (as I have done).

The great Saxon hymn "Now thank we all our God" has a similar background. Between 1620 and 1648, the Thirty Years War, Eilenburg in Saxony suffered appallingly. It was sacked three times. It had a great influx of refugees, and suffered four times from the plague. The population was decimated. Only one Minister survived, Martin Rinkart. When it was all over he wrote his masterpiece. He based it on Ecclesiasticus, that 'legacy of great value', whose story is told in its Preface. His inspiration was the passage beginning: "Now bless ye the God of all . . . " (Ch. 50:22). But once again it is not just another hymn; it is a reflection of a man's tried and tested personality recorded for posterity. Again, in worship, it should be introduced as such.

Central to any real Christian faith there has to be this sense of eternal gratitude.

29. MORE ABOUT THE SEA

Gratitude is not the only mark of the Christian, as this story will demonstrate.

For the past twenty years or so I have acted as a "Reader" at a small rural church in Anglesey, called "Llanallgo", conducting popular services and assisting at the Eucharist. Like other churches on the island it is a Celtic foundation, believed to date from the seventh century. But the event which made it famous occurred in 1859.

There was an appalling and totally unexpected storm. A magnificent vessel, the *Royal Charter*, had been just approaching Liverpool when it struck. The gentle breeze backed to the north east, becoming a howling gale. The ship had come from Melbourne. She was the last word in luxury. Her sails were supplemented by steam engines which by themselves would drive her at five knots. Unbelievably she had made the trip in two months! She carried a cargo of gold, and many of the passengers had found wealth in the Australian gold rush.

But in the face of the gale she was helpless. They lightened ship, chopped down the mast, tried to hold her with anchors, but it was all to no avail. She grounded on sharp rocks near Llanallgo Church, in pitch darkness, at low water. They got a landline ashore from the bows, but the first woman passenger panicked and held everyone up. Then the ship broke in halves, leaving all the other women and children in the after saloon. A readable and well-researched paperback, *The Golden Wreck*, by the late Alexander McKee, tells the whole story.

Only a handful of strong men survived. For months afterwards hideously battered bodies and limbs came ashore all along the coastline. Some of them had been weighted down with gold. There was a formal inquest, and a public inquiry. The scandal of the gold (some of which obviously got into wrong hands), and of the four or five hundred deaths, filled the newspapers for weeks. Llanallgo Church was stripped of its pews and fittings, and the bodies were taken there for identification and burial. There was trouble over space in the tiny graveyard, some multiple burials, and some bodies removed to an adjacent parish for burial there. Other bodies, washed up perhaps months later, and a long way from where it all happened, were buried in the nearest Parish churchyard. A memorial stone stands on the cliff top where the tragedy occurred.

The disaster happened on October 26, 1859. At that time Charles Dickens had just launched a current affairs periodical with a wide readership in Britain and North America. Just after Christmas he came up by train and spent a couple of days as the guest of the Rector. He wrote up the story, concentrating on the Rector's tireless efforts on behalf of the bereaved families who came from near and far. Soon the humble Rector was world-famous; but such had been the strain, he was dead within two years, a great man of God. The magazine was called *All the Year Round*, but readers today can find the article in the book called *The Uncommercial Traveller* (a pen-name which Dickens used).

Almost exactly eighteen hundred years previously there had been another wreck, which, in many ways, was exactly similar. A ship, with passengers and cargo, was caught up unexpectedly in a north easterly gale off the coast of Crete. It was carried along helplessly. The crew lightened the ship and tried to hold her with anchors, as with the *Royal Charter*. Eventually she was driven up against an island. But, unlike the later tragedy, everybody managed to scramble ashore before the vessel broke up. There is, not a memorial, but a statue at the point where it happened, to the man mainly responsible for the happy outcome. The island was Malta, the man's name was Paul. The story appears in Acts,

Ch. 27. It is quite extraordinary, because Paul was only a prisoner in the hold, guarded by soldiers. But he took control. The sheer force of his Christian personality, his refusal to panic, gave him authority. As Moses demonstrated many hundreds of years previously, when he led the Children of Israel through the wilderness, a truly godly person can sometimes have that natural authority in times of difficulty.

Our faith, if it is genuine, should give us a similar strength and courage at moments of crisis.

The church which Paul founded in Malta has existed without a break ever since. It is unique. Today the Cathedral is dedicated to Publius, who was the Roman Governor at the time; the cave in which Paul is said to have worshipped is nearby, and it contains a picture said to have been painted by Luke. There must have been later correspondence between Paul and his friends on the island, but it has all been lost. What a tragedy it is that we cannot today read in our scriptures the 'Epistles to the Maltese'!

30. FAMILY MATTERS

I was reading Chapter 5 of the Book of James. It starts off: "Go to, now, you rich men, weep and howl for the miseries that shall come upon you." Then it goes on: "Your gold and silver have rusted . . . "

Gold and silver. . . rusting . . . surely not! Gold does not rust; that is why it is used as the basis of money. I wrote in the last chapter about the wreck of the *Royal Charter*. There is still gold in the wreckage. It will be intact if ever it is found.

This is, in fact, a little point. The experts tell us that there is only one place in the whole wide world where gold rusts. That is in the thick, treacly waters of the Dead Sea. Therefore the Book of James was written in the vicinity of the Dead Sea. And what more likely place than Jerusalem?

Traditionally the Book of James was written by James the brother of Jesus. If that is so the book is a disappointment. James could have written so much about the boyhood of Jesus. We know so little about the time of Jesus' childhood. What a story there must be! What happened to Joseph? When Mary was widowed did Jesus as the eldest son have to take on the family responsibility? Did He run the carpenter's shop? And what was it that enabled Him to leave His home and commence His ministry? Perhaps James wrote about His home life on another scroll that has been lost. If so, what a tragedy!

What we have is a book that hardly mentions Jesus. It closely resembles in style the Apocryphal Book of Ecclesiasticus (the "Church Book"). It is full of commonsense, and contains much that a Christian will find helpful. It apparently comes to us from a strange Jewish church. Some Jews in Jerusalem accepted the truth about Jesus. Seemingly, their synagogue worship (there were many synagogues in Jerusalem) retained Jewish customs, such as circumcision, but had also embraced Christianity. It was an introspective form of Christianity, quite different from the world church envisaged by men like Paul. It probably disappeared with the fall of Jerusalem in 70 AD.

The book contains a miscellany of small points. James disliked snobbery. He compares the rich man arriving in church and being treated with deference, with the poor man who is told to 'stand there' or 'sit on the floor' (Ch. 2:3). It happens today! I can recall some instances in which the rich, because of their status and contribution, have expected to dominate church affairs, including sometimes what is said from the pulpit; it is a tendency that must be resisted, even at a price. But equally, rich and distinguished people can be a tremendous asset. My own village church has by the roadside what appears to be a large War Memorial; it is in fact a memorial to a privileged outsider who once lived in the big house nearby, and who was killed in the Boer War. The real communal memorial is a humble plaque inside the church.

James sees the tongue as one of our most important organs. It can do enormous harm, and enormous good. It is like a fire. It can start off as a tiny flame, and end up as an enormous conflagration. At the time of writing most people will have seen on television the fire at the Bradford City Football Ground. The flames seemed so insignificant when they started off in one corner. Within minutes the whole stand was ablaze from end to end. Guard that small flame, your tongue! The tongue is 'a little member, but boasts great things' (Ch. 3:5). James writes of a great ship; it is not the storm that directs it, but the small rudder at the stern. This is important teaching.

James makes many such points. But the one that has produced the most discussion is his repeated and emphasized theme, that "Faith without works is dead". How can a person with faith not respond to that faith with good works, knowing as he must the enormity of God's love and sacrifice for him through His Son? He is in any case lifted up by a power which comes from outside himself. Superficially, it is a contradiction in terms. But it seems to me that James is writing in practical terms about fallible human beings with an imperfect faith – such people are to be found in every church. I see no problem; indeed it is a lesson I need to take to heart. But Luther wanted this book to be excluded from the Canon of Scripture. I shall come back to this.

31. THE ROCK

James had a close companion in Jerusalem . . . Peter (Gal. 2:18-19). But of course Peter ended up in Rome, as we all know.

In the New Testament there are two short Epistles from Peter. They are well worth looking at, as one would expect.

Reading through the first of them, I come upon these works (1 Peter 5:13): "The church that is at Babylon . . . saluteth you; and so doth Marcus (Mark) my son." Babylon? Babylon was six hundred miles *east* of Jerusalem. It was where, five or six hundred years previously, the Jews had been exiled. It no longer existed, although today it is at last being reconstructed on its original site.

Peter obviously did not intend his readers to take him literally. Mark was his close companion, not his son. And the word 'Babylon' conjured up in Jewish minds a picture of a great, evil, materialistic city given over to idol worship. Rome, Peter was saying, resembles Babylon.

His Epistle is a stirring call to steadfastness among the Christian people scattered around the Roman empire. They had been redeemed with the precious blood of Christ. As newborn babes they were to desire the sincere milk of the word. They were a chosen generation, a royal priesthood, a holy nation, a peculiar (i.e. unique) people, They were to humble themselves and cast all their care upon the chief Shepherd. There is much more.

Scholars tell us that this Epistle was Peter's 'Baptismal Address'. In the Anglican Church, it would resemble the Bishop's address to the newly confirmed. In those days converts would usually have been adults. "Baptism" and "Confirmation" would normally then have been combined in a single ceremony.

There was, however, one great difference. We can read this Epistle, and benefit greatly from what we read; but the original readers were a bitterly persecuted minority. Their religious practices brought physical danger. They were discriminated against. Peter himself was crucified.

We perhaps say to ourselves on a Sunday morning: "I don't think I'll bother with Church. It's raining and the car's out of action . . ." We are casual. Whereas to those early Christians worship really meant something! And we wonder . . . how would our casual faith stand up if it were to be tested as theirs was? We cannot know the answer. We can only stand back and admire.

Peter's second Epistle brings us up with a jerk! In Chapter 1:14, we read: "Knowing that shortly I must put off this my tabernacle . . . ", and verse 15 uses the words: "after my decease". He is telling us that he is about to die. Paul in II Timothy, Chapter 4, uses similar words: "The time of my departure is at hand. I have fought a good fight, I have finished my course, I have kept the faith" (Verses 6–7). Paul is assumed to have been beheaded at about the same time. He writes without an iota of fear!

But we know that Peter's second Epistle is not quite what it appears to be. It was written about a century after the event. An unknown writer was deeply concerned about the heresies of his time. He decided that he would write in the style of Peter. It would have been like a modern writer assuming the personality and style of Dickens. There would have been no thought of deception; it was a legitimate literary device. He was writing for his own generation. He could not possibly have foreseen that nearly two thousand years later readers would still be reading his words and that they might find them confusing. Peter, he knew, would have displayed this sort of courage before his crucifixion!

In its call to holiness this Epistle contains (Ch. 1:5-8) a magnificent summary of what Christian behaviour should be. We have "great and precious gifts"; and we must "add to our faith, virtue, and to virtue, knowledge, and to knowledge, temperance, and to temperance, patience, and to patience, godliness, and to godliness, brotherly kindness, and to brotherly kindness, charity". 'Knowledge' in the Christian sense comes our way from life's experiences and from our devotions and studies. Modern versions use the expression 'self-control' instead of 'temperance'. 'Brotherly kindness' is the affection that one Christian bears towards another. 'Love' represents our attitude towards the whole human race. These are words to think about, again against the background of Peter's immense courage.

32. REBIRTH.

Earlier in this book I have written of the way in which those who come to accept the truth of Jesus Christ find the inward peace of mind which

He promised at the Last Supper and which Paul clearly found after his experience on the Damascus Road. But there is a paradox.

To the ordinary man in his natural state sin does not mean very much. But a person who believes, who reads his Bible and who meditates, becomes aware of the enormity of the sacrifice which God's own Son made on the Cross. It is something he cannot escape. He acquires a sense of guilt. He cannot possibly aspire to serve such a God. He is human and imperfect. His every weakness crucifies God again. There is no hope for him.

Now in the year 1738 there was an extraordinary event concerned with the Holy Spirit, one that has inspired hundreds of millions of Christian people since. It was John Wesley's conversion.

John Wesley was a priest in the Church of England. He was middle-aged. He wanted desperately to succeed in his vocation. He drove himself mercilessly. Yet he felt himself to be an utter failure. He had an overwhelming sense of his own guilt.

In March of 1738 he was at crisis point. He had tried unsuccessfully to be a missionary. But now he was about to give up the ministry he so much loved.

He had a good friend who belonged to the small but highly respected Moravian Church. From him he received two pieces of advice. Firstly he was to 'purge his philosophies', as I have already mentioned. But secondly he was to 'preach faith until he had faith'. He thought about this through Lent and beyond.

On May 24th he got up and read his New Testament in Greek at 5.00 a.m., his regular practice. It demonstrates how he was driving himself; in fact, although he did not realise it, he was trying to be a Minister of the Gospel in his own strength. Later in the day he attended Evensong at St. Paul's, where, again as I have mentioned earlier, the Psalm started with the words "Out of the depths I cry unto Thee". Of what happened in the evening he wrote: "I went very unwillingly to a society in Aldersgate Street, where one was reading Luther's preface to the Epistle to the Romans . . . he was describing the change which God works in the heart through faith in Christ . . . I felt my heart strangely warmed . . . I felt I did trust in Christ, Christ alone, for salvation. He had taken away my sins and saved me from the law of sin and death."

Luther's preface, which inspired Wesley on that fateful evening, reads in part: "I stood before God as a sinner troubled in conscience . . . I did not love a just and angry God. Night and day I pondered until I saw the connection between the justice of God and the statement that 'The just shall live by his faith'. Then I grasped that the justice of God is that righteousness by which through grace and mercy God justifies us through faith . . . I felt myself to be reborn. This passage of Paul became to me a gate to heaven."

The Authorised Version quotes Luther's Text as: " . . . as it is written, the just shall live by faith" (Romans 1:17 part). John Wesley would have studied it in the original Greek. Paul himself wrote, elsewhere in Romans: "O wretched man that I am! Who shall deliver me from the body of this death?" These are strong words, suggesting that he too had suffered a crisis of conscience. I think that to these three great Christian men, Wesley, Luther and Paul, it was like diving into a deep ocean from the side of a ship, and finding themselves buoyed up by the waters, the grace that comes through faith. They suddenly saw how it was that God (through Jesus) had demonstrated his incredible love for us all. He could not possibly have made it more obvious. Such a God is not out to condemn or destroy us, dreadful people though we may have been. He wants the very best for us. He wants to build us up, not punish us. He is a Father, like the father who had a prodigal son, and His instincts are those of a parent.

Depressive illness can be a desperately serious matter. One has the greatest respect for the professional psychiatrists who have to look for cures. But here we have the divine, not the human, answer.

Wesley was a trained Anglican clergyman, and Luther was a trained Roman priest. Romans is probably Paul's greatest Epistle. It is difficult reading. But the Jews were trying in their own strength to obey over six hundred religious laws, and failing. For the ordinary Christian here and now it boils down to faith and trust, simply accepting (and responding to) the incredible love which God bears towards us, fallible human beings that we are. We simply cannot possibly repay Him for the love demonstrated in His suffering – we should just accept in faith. We should be as little children, spontaneous in our responses, in our reaction to God's presence within us.

In June the new Wesley preached the first of the sermons which were to have such a tremendous effect. It was before a university congregation in Oxford. His Text was: "By Grace are you saved through faith", from Ephesians 2 – see my earlier Chapter on this Epistle. This Chapter encapsulates our relationship with God. We cannot buy salvation by our own good works, any more than we can lift ourselves up with our own shoe-laces!

Subconsciously or consciously, that is what many if not most of us are trying to do! And people who claim that they are 'as good as those who go to church' completely miss the point, don't they!

SIXTH EXCURSION. THE OLD CITY

Preacher looks at The Old Testament, at Habakuk the gentle musician, at Elijah, Elisha, Amos and Hosea, the Prophets of the Lost Tribe of Israel, at Isaiah, Jeremiah, Ezekiel and Deutero-Isaiah, the Prophets of Judah, and at Ruth and Daniel.

33. ROOTS

Did you notice the words 'as it is written' in the quotation from Romans which I have just mentioned? Paul was actually quoting from a 'Minor Prophet' who had lived hundreds of years before his time.

But I wish they wouldn't use the expression 'Minor Prophet'. The Old Testament concludes with twelve short books of prophesy. Because they are short they are called 'minor'. Some of them are works by truly great and loveable men. It is one such from whom Paul was quoting.

In the reign of Josiah in the seventh century BC, there was a religious revival. The inhabitants of Judah did what was right in the sight of the Lord. But they were constantly threatened by the big powers coming in from the north. Josiah himself was killed in battle at Armageddon. It was an evil which would not go away. In the end it destroyed them.

There lived at that time a gentle, devoted musician, a man of harmony, whom we know simply by his nickname, Habakkuk, which means, 'Embracer'. He left us three short chapters. Why, he asked himself, should they suffer misfortune when they didn't deserve to? To us today it is a common human experience. Those who lead virtuous lives often die young and suffer numerous misfortunes; we see it as a part of that eternity in which the real rewards lie. With rich insight Habakkuk conceived the phrase: "The just shall live by his faith" (Ch. 2:4).

The good man is not shielded from misfortune, but has within himself that faith which enables him to rise above whatever may happen to him.

Misfortune is part of the discipline of life. Faith enables us to live through our misfortunes and to overcome them. When the singer Kathleen Ferrier, with her superb voice and lovely personality, was cruelly smitten by cancer, she didn't give way to misery. She fractured a limb on stage, and carried on; nobody in the audience knew what had happened. She was an inspiration to all, right to the end. That is what 'the just living by faith' meant to Habakkuk (literally, "the righteous by his steadfastness liveth" – Young's Literary Translation).

Although the words went much deeper as far as Paul was concerned (see the Epistle to the Romans) he, deliberately, because of his calling, lived a life which in worldly terms was that of a failure. With his talents he could have been a successful businessman or a top administrator (he had Roman citizenship). He could have been a respected citizen leading a life of affluence and comfort. Instead he suffered endless hardship, ending in premature death by execution. But that was what gave him real satisfaction, because it was the way of faith and joy. The other way would have made him miserable. Again, it was 'the just living by faith' as Habakkuk meant it.

Chapter 3 of the Book begins with the words: "A prayer of Habakkuk the prophet upon Shigioneth", and it ends with: "To the chief singer on my stringed instruments". Habakkuk was the musical director. This chapter is poetry, not prose, intended for singing. It is one of the most beautiful passages in the Old Testament. It describes all the evils that can come upon us . . . yet, it concludes, 'I will rejoice in the Lord, I will joy in the God of my salvation' . . . living by faith! "Upon Shigioneth" means "To the music of the Psalms of ecstasy". The Hebrew words had a haunting, rapidly changing, exciting rhythm, associated with David and his psalms. Habakkuk could only possibly do justice to his theme through poetry and music!

34. DROUGHT

And so, back in time, from the seventh to the ninth century BC, to the prophet Elijah, starting with a story . . .

There was a terrible drought. There had been no rain for three years. Animals, and human beings, were dying. What could possibly have been the cause of all this misery? Was it the fault of Baal, or was it the fault of the God of Elijah? King Ahab decided that the matter must be put to the test.

They gathered on a mountain-side. Firstly the priests of Baal were to appear. They were to take a bullock, cut it up, lay it on wood, and call down fire from heaven. They proceeded, and for a whole morning called upon their god, leaping and cutting themselves with knives; but nothing happened. Then Elijah, the Prophet of the One True God, took over. He took his bullock, and cut it up. Then he set up an altar of twelve stones, representing the twelve tribes of Israel. Then he dug a deep trench around it, and put his bullock on top of the wood provided. Then he ordered that four barrels of water be poured into the trench, followed by another four, and then four again. He prayed to the One True God; fire came and consumed the sacrifice, and the wood, and the stones, and the water.

But just a minute . . . there had been a prolonged drought . . . everything was parched and dry . . . water? What water? I shall explain later.

When Solomon had died, many years previously, the kingdom of Israel became a battlefield. With his grandiose schemes, Solomon had placed a great burden on his people, and this was the result. Eventually the tribe of Judah broke away and became a little separate nation centred on Jerusalem, while the remaining Israelis occupied the country to the north known as Samaria. Elijah, the prophet about whom I am writing, lived in Israel as it then was, without the one tribe of Judah. It became what we know as 'the lost tribe of Israel', but of that later. His King was Ahab, depicted as a weak man dominated by an evil wife, Jezebel, who worshipped Baal. She died the death she deserved, when she fell from a window and dogs devoured her remains. Elijah was 'a hairy man'; John the Baptist imitated his style of dress, and when Jesus was transfigured on the mountain top this man Elijah appeared as the one who represented the prophets, He is an important figure. He was followed in Israel by Elisha, who was bald; Elisha was taunted by children who shouted "Baldy, Baldy" after him. Children at least have not changed very much!

But back to the story of the sacrifices on the mountain-side. The prophets of Baal and all their families were killed. The One True God having assumed His rightful place among the people, the drought now came to an end. There was a 'cloud no bigger than a man's fist', followed soon by a deluge. But Jezebel swore that Elijah would die for what he had done.

Elijah, depressed and disheartened, and feeling quite alone, ran away in a blind panic. He made for the border of Judah, crossed it, and went as far south as he could, to the town of Beersheba – beyond that there is only desert and mountain country. There he found a cave in the side of the sacred Mount Horeb, the same range as that in which Moses had found the Ten Commandments. While he was there God came to him. God was not in the wind which broke the stones. He was not in the earthquake that followed. He was not in the fire, which followed again. He was in the stillness that followed the deluge, the 'still, small voice'. God gave Elijah faith and confidence again, told him he was by no means alone, and told him what he must do next. Like many a modern Christian, he found his courage and his mission by listening to the tiny voice that speaks to us when we pray. We must listen for it, mustn't we!

The water? If my readers look for Mount Carmel on the map, they will find that it slopes down to the sea. The water was sea water!

35. THE LOST TRIBE

Amos prophesied about a hundred years after Elijah, in the eighth century BC. Unlike Elijah, he was not actually a native of Israel. He was a herdsman at Tekoa, in Judah, a man used to the wide open spaces. He was also a man with a deep social concern. He did not like what he saw in neighbouring Israel. The ruling classes were pampered, corrupt and rotten. The poor were oppressed and often robbed of what little they had. There was evil and wickedness everywhere.

So he travelled north across the border and into Bethel. Jacob had been there a thousand years previously. God had spoken to him through his dream about the ladder, and he had set up an altar there. The altar had now become an elaborate Chapel Royal. But true religion had disappeared. This was a place given over to empty ritual and sacrifice. Modern churches can, and sometimes do, make the same mistake. They can lose their way by becoming obsessed with the wrong things.

Amos' speech was blunt and picturesque. In a sense it resembled that of John Bunyan. He described the rich women as 'fat cows'. He was abusive, very abusive, towards the Chief Priest. The result was that he was deported.

The Book of Amos, two thousand eight hundred years old, is said to be the oldest in the Bible. The Chief Priest had him deported to keep him quiet. Probably that was why his words were written down, and have survived to this very day!

But the other natural human prophet of the Lost Tribe was Hosea, a much more likeable person than Amos (Elijah and Elisha are hardly 'natural' and 'human' in view of the miracles with which they are associated). Unlike Amos he was a native, a man who loved his country and everything about it. He too could see the corruption and the persecution, and it saddened him. Successive leaders were assassinated, a measure of the sort of government they had. Bands of robbers were actually organised by the priests, the men who were supposed to be providing the moral leadership. Yet these were God's Chosen People!

Hosea's sadness was reflected in his own private life. He writes about it with a decent restraint. Seemingly he loved an exquisitely beautiful dancer called Gomer, and married her. But she was faithless and promiscuous. The children she bore were not his. Eventually she left him altogether. Years later he found her again, ugly, almost unrecognisable, riddled, we presume, with sexually related disease. She was a slave, being sold off cheaply. He bought her back.

Hosea felt he could just begin to understand God's love towards His people, because it was so much like his own towards Gomer, but on a much, much higher plain. It was the incredibly wonderful sort of love which later led God's own Son to sacrifice Himself in death. Hosea's prophesy is emotional, written in short jerky sentences. It is poetical. It is often self-contradictory; "God will forgive His people", and "Punishment will certainly come". He is a sad yet loveable person, who, later, was quoted with obvious respect by Jesus during His ministry. His words also appear in the Epistles and elsewhere in the New Testament. He has much to teach us. He was a great man.

The corrupt and rotten nation brought upon itself its own downfall, as Hosea had foreseen. Israel was conquered and overrun. Samaria the capital fell in 721 BC. Many of the inhabitants were either killed or driven out of the country. Some may have escaped to Judah. Those remaining were joined by a mixture of races, Assyrian colonists and others, and they became the despised 'Samaritans' of Jesus' day. Israel's neighbour, little Judah, was now alone in a hostile world, with its border to the north wide open to predators.

Far-fetched legends exist about the Lost Tribe of Israel, which is said to have reappeared in other extremely unlikely places. It all happened so very long ago that I cannot believe that there is any truth in any of them.

36. THE REMNANT
During the last century two ministers, close friends, met at a conference.

One, very sad, had just lost his only daughter. What could the other man possibly say when faced with that kind of situation? Words seemed useless. He said simply: "By these things men live."

In fact this rather trite remark is a text. In those days ministers all used certain standard texts; this one comes from Isaiah (Ch. 38:16), and would have been familiar. It conjured up a truly remarkable story.

Judah was now alone. Isaiah was a senior adviser to a number of successive kings who reigned in Jerusalem, its capital. The event referred to took place during the reign of Hezekiah, the good and quite remarkable monarch who saw during his reign the fall of Israel.

To simplify history a little (as I am doing throughout these stories of the prophets), Judah was now threatened by the Assyrian host, armed to the teeth and utterly ruthless. Their leader was Sennacherib, whom they first attempted to bribe. But there was also feverish activity within Jerusalem. The walls were repaired and strengthened. The most vulnerable section, to the north, was doubled. Food was stored in readiness for a possibly long siege. But . . . what were they to do about water? Their supply came from a well outside the city walls.

The way they solved that problem is quite extraordinary. They built a five-hundred-yard tunnel from their well to what became the Pool of Siloam within enlarged city walls. It went through solid rock, and was just big enough for a man stooping slightly to walk through. One can imagine the darkness, and the primitive tools which they used. How on earth did they do it? But they did! They left an inscription in Hebrew, carved into the rock at the Siloam end, which described what they had done.

They were just in time. According to Isaiah, Sennacherib arrived and laid siege to the city. They looked out over the walls, day after day and week after week, and the soldiers were still there. Then an amazing thing happened. I quote Isaiah: "Then the angel of the Lord went forth, and smote in the camp of the Assyrians a hundred and fourscore and five thousand: and when they arose early in the morning, behold, they were all dead corpses." To make sense of the language, obviously the first 'they' refers to the defenders, and the second to the Assyrian army. It is true historically that Sennacherib withdrew and never again attacked Jerusalem. A possible explanation is that the Assyrian soldiers were smitten by the plague, so common in those days, perhaps brought by mice. To the inhabitants of Jerusalem it was quite simply a miracle from above, designed to protect God's Holy City.

But Isaiah goes on to tell us that this was not the whole of Hezekiah's troubles. I have been writing about Chapter 37. Chapter 38 tells us that Hezekiah became sick unto death; Isaiah said to him: "Set thine house in order: for thou shalt die, and not live." Hezekiah 'prayed'; and Hezekiah 'wept sore'. God responded through His prophet: "I have heard thy prayer, I have seen thy tears: behold, I will add unto thy days fifteen years." The prophet had said: "Let them take a lump of figs, and lay it as a plaister (sic) upon the boil (the cause of the sickness), and he shall recover." In his prayer of thanksgiving Hezekiah used the words of the text: "By these things men live". He had survived so very much!

The lesson for us all is that we should be patient and persistent, despite the misfortunes that come our way. Let us hope that the bereaved minister found some comfort in the story.

But this was not the end of the matter as far as little Judah was concerned, as we shall see.

37. DISASTER

In the prophesy of Jeremiah, Chapter 32, verses 9 onwards, the prophet tells us: "I bought the field at Anathoth from my cousin Hanamel and weighed out the price, seventeen shekels of silver. I signed and sealed the Deed and had it witnessed; then I weighed out the money on the scales. I took my copies of the deed of purchase, both the sealed and the unsealed, and gave them to Baruch son of Neriah, son of Mahseiah, in the presence of Hanamel my cousin, of the witnesses whose names were on the deed of purchase, and of the Judaeans sitting in the court of the guard-house. In the presence of them all I gave my instructions to Baruch: 'These are the words of the Lord of Hosts the God of Israel: Take these copies of the deed of purchase, the sealed and the unsealed, and deposit them in an earthenware jar so that they may be preserved for a long time.'"

That reminds me of the interesting experience I had when we bought our present house. It involved the Halifax Building Society, the Midland Bank, and a local Estate Agent and Solicitor . . . but just a minute! We are supposed to be talking about religion. Jeremiah was *preaching* when he told us all this. What on earth was he getting at?

To find our explanation, we must go back ten years, to the year 597 BC (Hezekiah had belonged to the eighth century BC). Jeremiah lived in Jerusalem. In that year the city was besieged by Nebuchadnezzar and his Babylonian army, and defeated. Prominent citizens, including the young king and the temple priest Ezekiel, were taken to Babylon as hostages. A puppet ruler, Zedekiah, was appointed to govern Judah. But he proved to be a weak and vacillating leader, foolishly defying the Babylonians who had put him there, and perpetually seeking alliances with the other great power, Egypt. In 594 BC he was summoned to Babylon to explain himself. It made no difference. Nebuchadnezzar eventually and predictably came on a punitive expedition. Jerusalem fell in 587 BC.

Jeremiah's message throughout had been that they should remain loyal to Babylon. Increasingly he was accused of treachery. He was imprisoned. He was thrown into a pit, from which friends rescued him in the nick of time. But still he persisted. He described their likely fate in vivid terms, such as when he likened them to a flawed piece of pottery in the potter's hands – the potter simply destroyed his work and started from scratch. Their religion veered towards idolatry. They took over the homes of the hostages, simply assuming that they would never return.

They believed that, however badly they behaved, God would protect His Holy City, as He had for Hezekiah nearly two centuries before.

They were sadly shaken in their belief when Nebuchadnezzar's army arrived. As they looked over the ramparts during the eighteen months of the siege they became more and more desperate. The famine and the hunger became unbearable. They thought now of their own history, how, some six hundred years previously, their ancestors had conquered the Promised Land. They had slaughtered all the citizens of Jericho and Ai. What a magnificent achievement it had been – but now the boot was on the other foot. They died a thousand deaths as in imagination they tried desperately to hide from the soldiers in their last moments.

And Jeremiah, there, with them, bought a field. It was quite impossible for him to inspect his new piece of real estate; Anathoth was seven or eight miles north of the city. But here was his act of faith in the future. It would not be as bad as their imagination had led them to suppose. That was the meaning of his message. They would, most of them, survive somehow. Eventually they would repossess the land.

In the event most of them did survive. Many ended up in exile in Babylon. King Zedekiah's sons were slaughtered in front of his eyes, and then his eyes were gouged out. Jerusalem itself was laid waste. Solomon's temple was utterly destroyed. Jeremiah told the people: "I will write my laws in their inward parts." There would be no temple to go to, no temple priests to guide them. He spoke of a "new covenant" (or "new testament" – the word is the same), words which have their echo when Jesus at the Last Supper used them ("the New Covenant of my Blood"), in connection with the wine which He offered to the apostles, suggesting the inward guidance of the Holy Spirit.

Even the darkest cloud has its silver lining: things are rarely quite as bad as our fevered imagination might make them out to be. The truly godly man keeps his head in times of stress. After I had been talking along these lines in a service, a worshipper wrote to me. She described how a young bride, at the beginning of the Second World War, had found herself alone and lonely. She had occupied herself by buying up beautiful antiques, which could be obtained very cheaply. It had been a sensible distraction – like Jeremiah's purchase of the field – because when it was all over she and her husband were able to enjoy these lovely things which normally they could never have afforded. It was the attitude, not the action in itself, which was important.

While Jeremiah was prophesying in Jerusalem, the temple priest Ezekiel was delivering a similar message in Babylon. There is a similar sorrow behind his vividly descriptive words. Like Jeremiah, he has much to teach us.

Jeremiah had a hard time of it, but how about Ezekiel, watching it all from six hundred miles away? He had been trained for the service of the Temple and the people; instead he had to watch from a distance as the religious faith of his people deteriorated. In Babylon the news came that the people in Jerusalem had taken and occupied the homes of Ezekiel and his fellow hostages; imagine their feelings! Then Ezekiel's wife died. But as the gifted and imaginative man that he was, Ezekiel persisted in his God-inspired message, despite the worry and sorrow. He left us some gems of imagination, such as the famous stories of the valley of the dry bones and of the good ship *Tyre*. In the latter he likened the city of Tyre, which was almost surrounded by water, to a superb ship. It was made of the most beautiful materials, carried the costliest of cargoes, and had a talented crew. But it sank without trace! Tyre, with all its wealth and materialism, was like that. When I used this story in a service, the comment I had at the door was: "Things haven't changed much, have they?"

These linked prophesies teach us one thing. We who are preachers will never find a perfect background for what we are trying to do. There are always adverse factors. Despite that, we must *enjoy* what we are doing! Jeremiah and Ezekiel lived through dreadful times. It is debatable which one suffered most. But their words come down to us as imaginative masterpieces, and we can all profit by studying their vivid teaching.

I am reminded of the time during the war years which I spent in Durban. I met a white South African called George Fish, and our friendship lasted through many years. He was a Local Preacher and a prominent member of the Boy Scout movement. Living as he did against a background of racial discrimination he fought constantly to bring black and white together in fellowship by arranging scout activities, and he took as his basic principle the idea that, in his words, 'the whole notion of a chosen people belongs to the Old Testament. The essence of all Christian belief is, in this respect, that there is neither Jew nor Greek, male or female, bond or free, but that all humanity is on one level in the sight of God'. He failed in his message in the sense that the extremes of apartheid were to come later, with the 1948 National Party government, but, like Jeremiah and Ezekiel, he said and he did what he believed to be right, from within South Africa, and with understanding.

38. STRANGE WORDS

At the end of Chapter 40 in Isaiah's prophesy I read some very strange words indeed (as I shall explain): "Even the youths shall faint and be weary, and the young men shall utterly fall: But they that wait upon the Lord shall renew their strength; they shall mount up with wings as eagles; they shall run, and not be weary; and they shall walk, and not faint." This is part of the message of the so-called "Deutero-Isaiah", who has no connection with the Isaiah who advised Hezekiah ('Isaiah' in our Bible is really two books joined together).

After the fall of Jerusalem in 587 BC many Jews settled in Babylon; we believe that about three thousand of them made the long trip as prisoners-of-war. Babylon was the great city built by Nebuchadnezzar. They created what we would call a 'ghetto'. They were not really happy, although through the years many of them seemed to prosper, with successful businesses and other activities. Children were born and old people died. Some married outside their race. Their Hebrew language was no use to them. When they sang: "How shall we sing the Lord's song in a strange land?" (Psalm 137:4) they certainly had in mind the superbly beautiful rhythm of their Hebrew psalms, quite impossible to translate.

Some fifty years later this 'Deutero-Isaiah' became their leader, inspiring them with his words much as Winston Churchill did with us through the war years. Also, events outside took an unpredictable turn. The Babylonian masters were defeated by the Persians. The great liberal King Cyrus of Persia took over the city without any fighting. The Persian dynasty founded by Cyrus lasted for two thousand five hundred years. The late Shah of Persia was the last in the succession, and many will remember the celebration that he arranged to mark the anniversary. Cyrus discovered that in his treasury in Babylon there were gold and silver vessels. On inquiry he was told that they had been taken from the Jewish Temple in Jerusalem. Looking further into the matter, he issued his famous decree, that the Jews should re-establish themselves in their own land. Jeremiah's prophesy, belatedly, was being fulfilled!

We can imagine the debate. Some Jews would have given verbal support to the idea, but their roots were now firmly in Babylon. And what an undertaking! A six-hundred-mile journey westward across inhospitable desert, then a drop down to the Jordan valley. Then they would have to cross the river somehow (no Allenby Bridge in those days!), and climb up four thousand feet on the other side. And what then? A heap of rat-infested rubble, with perhaps a few settlers living in shanty town conditions, untouched for fifty years! It is one of the wonders of history that the Jews did repossess their land. It took many years. They rebuilt Jerusalem in a hostile environment. They established, not a kingdom as before, but a theocratic state, a state run by the Church like that created by the Pilgrim Fathers in New England.

But why did I call the text 'very strange'? Had you noticed? It seems to be back to front! The young men were to fly like eagles, they were to run and not be weary, but finally they were to walk and not faint. The first expedition of strong young men, making that awful journey back, would need, above all, persistence. Nobody can run for six hundred miles! This adventure was going to take a long time. Then, with God's help, it would be possible.

We all know, don't we, those people on church committees who are always full of ambitious ideas, but who, somehow, when it comes to action, soon give up. It is the same with every worthwhile ambition; the real achievers are those with unspectacular persistence. We must be like them! That is why Deutero-Isaiah's words are as they are.

In connection with 'Deutero-Isaiah', when I read his words from the New English Bible, I sometimes conclude with the remark: "I knew the man who wrote this." I mean, of course, the translator, not the prophet himself, as I hasten to explain! It brings back a precious memory. Christopher North was a renowned scholar whose work on this particular prophet brought him considerable fame. He was also a friend, who would comment constructively and kindly on my efforts from the pulpit. But one tiny incident has remained firmly in my mind. He was unable to attend a service which I was planned to conduct, and, fearing that his absence would be misunderstood, he took the trouble to telephone me and explain the circumstances. So often, it is the little things that matter, isn't it!

I have summarised some of the stories of the prophets, taking them in historical order (apart from Habakkuk). Readers will have noticed that there are many worthwhile lessons to be taught and learned. Properly understood, their words are superb – but, more than that, it is the men behind the words, and the way they coped, that provides the real inspiration. With each prophet I have tried to arouse the interest and curiosity of listeners in the first few words. As in all my preaching, worshippers at the door afterwards have told me about their own experiences in the biblical places mentioned, for example, how they have actually travelled from Babylon to Jerusalem in modern times.

But with our modern congregations it is a great mistake to read without explanation passages from the writings of these men, as so often happens. Reading Chapter 1 of Ezekiel to a Eucharist congregation I noticed that two little boys in the front were entranced – this was real space-age stuff! But I suspect it meant very little to the older people. Background knowledge is, I repeat, so important. In any case, in this respect, I enjoy greatly the freedom of an ordinary, chapel service, in which one can follow through a theme with an imaginative selection of passages from all parts of the Bible.

39. A QUESTION OF RACE

Apart from the prophets, the Old Testament can provide endless inspiration. I offer just two stories . . .

It was a Bank Holiday Sunday. I had a packed congregation at a popular seaside resort in Welsh Wales. Before the service I had been told that there were Germans present; their relatives had been in a major earthquake in southern Italy, but had survived without a scratch.

I gave thanks for their deliverance in the prayers. Then, after the service, when I was speaking to the worshippers at the door, a man with a guttural accent shook me by the hand. "Ah," I said, "you must be one of the Germans."

His response took me completely off balance. "Don't insult me," the man said, "I'm a Pole. You know nothing." He went on to explain his bitter hatred for the Germans. I realised that he must have been one of the Polish refugees living in that part of the world. I could not judge him. It simply reminded me of the bitterness that still exists in continental Europe. I thought of another European friend, an artist and a Belgian Jew, who missed the gas chambers by a hair's breadth. The Pole was right; I know nothing!

This led me to concoct a story. I thought of a Polish mother and father, with their two sons, who escaped to Lleyn and settled in a Welsh community. The two sons, in the course of time, married two Welsh girls. They were all happy, until, unpredictably, bitter misfortune came their way. The three men all died, one after the other.

The ageing Polish mother, frail and weak, a lonely alien in a strange country, found to her joy that it would be possible for her to return to Poland. One of the daughters-in-law, for the sake of her beloved dead husband, saw that the old lady could not possibly go by herself; so she sacrificed herself. She accompanied her mother-in-law back to Poland.

Of course, in Poland there were no Calvinistic Methodist Chapels, no Cymanfa Ganu's (singing festivals). The language was foreign, the customs were strange. She had to fit in with a traditional Catholic church, in a Marxist setting. But, from sheer love, she made the best of it. She cared for the one who had become her responsibility. And, in the course of time, she married again, to a native Pole.

Now this is not really a modern story. It is the ancient story of Ruth, in a modern guise. Desperately hungry and weak from exhaustion the family from Bethlehem, the mother Naomi, the father, and the two sons, had like the Poles been forced to abandon their home. They had scrambled deep down into the valley of the Jordan, thousands of feet below. They had waded across the river, and with a superhuman effort had somehow climbed up the mountain-side to the east, to the land of Moab. They found food. They settled. The two sons found wives. Then the two of them, and their father, had all died. The aged Naomi was left alone. Ruth, one of her two daughters-in-law, accompanied her back to Bethlehem. She settled into an utterly strange and alien environment, And she actually remarried into Naomi's family.

The end of the story is that Ruth, the foreigner, had a son, and became King David's great grandmother, and an ancestor to Joseph, the natural father of Jesus. I like to think that she might have lived long enough to have seen the birth of Jesse, David's father.

We can be sure that the racial tensions in those far off days were just as great as they are in modern Europe. And refugees from famine are a familiar feature of our modern world.

This is, so far as I know, the only place in scripture which acknowledges the particular truth, that the younger generation has a family responsibility towards the old. We know that many wonderful people, especially single women, have devoted long years to the care of aged parents or parents-in-law. What unsung saints of God they are! Like 'famous men', they too deserve praise!

40. MORE ABOUT TENSIONS

There was a pagan idol, which every day demanded large quantities of food and drink. This was left daily in its temple by the worshippers. The following day it had always disappeared. More had to be provided.

'Superman' was sceptical. So he said to the king: "Seal the door with your seal, and see then whether the food disappears." The king did so.

The next day they broke the seal and went in. The food had disappeared! But 'superman' said: "Wait. Last night I scattered ashes on the floor. Come and look." Sure enough, there were many footsteps in the ashes. They led to a hidden hatch under a table. An underground passage then led out into the open air. The pagan priests and their families had removed the food!

The idol was Bel, a Babylonian god. The story is set in Babylon during the time of the Jewish exile, the sixth century BC. 'Superman' was Daniel. This is one of the six "Daniel" stories recorded in the Old Testament and in the Apocrypha. The writing on the wall, the three Hebrew servants in the burning fiery furnace, Daniel in the lion's den, are all superbly written stories in the same group. They are all set in Babylon. 'Superman', representing the virtue of the true Hebrew religion, always comes out victorious, sometimes by spectacular means. The 'goodies' always win!

Scholars believe that these stories come from the second century BC. Babylonian names and places from history are used much as we might use the names of Robin Hood or King Arthur in similar circumstances.

But the stories had a much more serious purpose.

Around 167 BC the Jews were involved in a bloody war with a Greek tyrant called Antiochus Epiphanus (the 'Super-human Being' from Antioch in Syria!). He hurt them where it hurt most, by trying to destroy the religion on which their whole culture was based. The Second Book of Maccabees is perhaps an exaggerated account, but the events it describes are hair-raising. All the Jewish religious practices had been banned. The temple was desecrated, the altar piled high with disgusting offerings, and the licentious revelry within its sacred walls included having sexual relationships with prostitutes. Two mothers who had their babies circumcised were led through the city and with their babies flung from the walls. Jews assembled together in a cave for their Sabbath worship were burned alive. Ninety-year-old Eleazar was killed for refusing to eat pork. A mother had to watch her seven sons being tortured and killed one after the other, before dying herself.

The 'Daniel' stories were intended to encourage the Jews in their defence of their religion. In the stories 'Superman Daniel' may have survived, but the reality was different. Thousands lost their lives in bitter fighting. Miraculously, the Jews won. The Temple, and their religious practices, were restored.

In the most famous episode of all, Daniel defied the pagan monarch by saying his prayers in public. Today we are not persecuted for our beliefs, but none the less like them we have sometimes to make a firm stand. Those who have served in the armed forces know that there is no privacy, even for the most intimate part of their faith. Generally, it is embarrassing, but is treated with respect by non-believers. Recently I conducted a service in a sparsely attended chapel. At the door I found to my surprise that my congregation had included a leading Methodist churchman, now retired. "Do you remember," he said, "forty-five years ago you and I were together in barracks? I have never forgotten the witness we made together when we made our devotions. It influenced me. I became a Minister and ended up a District Chairman." I had not recognised him and had forgotten; but we renewed our friendship that evening. In less serious vein, I recall the Sunday morning when we signalled Base from our ship: "Please send boat for church party." The reply came back: "Church party is not required from HMS . . . this morning." In the Services 'Church' was 'laid on' like everything else; nobody could imagine that anybody would actually *want* to go! Similarly several of us were forbidden to attend a sad memorial service because we had just given blood transfusions and would not be able to swing our arms as we marched! And I remember the day when, quite unnecessarily, I was refused permission to conduct a Service in the city in which we were based!

When it becomes necessary, in all sorts of different ways, Christians must be rigid in their refusal to compromise their beliefs.

It is perhaps ironic, that the persecutor of the Jews in this instance came from Antioch in Syria. Two hundred years later this was the city in which the word 'Christian' was first used!

SEVENTH EXCURSION. THE CONCERT HALL

Preacher looks at the musical side, the Old Testament psalms and Christian hymns.

41. THE GREATEST OF THE OLD

David the psalmist was also Israel's greatest king. He was Jesse's youngest son, and was brought up on a large farm in Bethlehem. He was the shepherd boy. How did he come to write his greatest psalm?

We read in scripture about King Saul's battles with the Philistines. The Philistines included in their ranks a giant of a man called Goliath, universally feared. We all learned when we were very young how the boy David slew Goliath on the battlefield, bringing a bloody victory to his own side (1 Samuel 17). Rereading the passage as adults we may reach a slightly modified conclusion about the story. David may be the hero, but he also begins to come across as an arrogant young man. "I" slew the bear and the lion with my own hands, "I" will kill the Philistine. He was such a gifted young man – after all, he was destined to become Israel's greatest leader. At that age it was natural. His pride undoubtedly grew as success came his way. He was a handsome young musician and singer. On the battlefield he met with success after success. He would have been mobbed by the young women on his return, like a modern 'pop' star. They began to make adverse comparisons between his success and Saul's relative failure (1 Samuel 18:7).

But Saul *was* the king. One day this conceited youth was playing his guitar-like instrument in the presence of Saul, and Saul could stand it no more. Something snapped; he lunged at the boy with a javelin (1 Samuel 19:10). There was nothing for it. The king was after David's blood. David had to run away.

The story of the relationship between Saul and David from then on is a complicated one. It can be found in the First Book of Samuel. Saul envied David and wanted to destroy him. The quarrel ended up in the inhospitable 'wilderness', which is frequently mentioned in scripture. In this case it meant the dry parched mountain side which sloped down into the depths of the earth to the Jordan valley and the Dead Sea two thousand feet below sea level. Suddenly, David had become unwanted. His whole life had collapsed about him. He was miserable. Youth sees this sort of experience in black and white terms, up in the skies or down in the depths. Older people know that there is a silver lining, that events have a way of straightening themselves out. This happened to David. He was reconciled with the king at a place called Engedi.

In his middle age David had a far worse experience. He had by then established himself as king in Jerusalem. He had a son called Absalom; the boy was what we would call a 'layabout'. Absalom organised a revolt against his father. David was forced out of Jerusalem. He went to the Mount of Olives, that scene of later sadness, and there he wept, grown man though he was. He was heartbroken . . . that the son whom he loved could behave in such a despicable way! Psalm 3 refers to this bad time. Of course, with his experience, the revolt was bound to fail. There was a great battle. Twenty thousand men lost their lives. What a terrible human tragedy it all was! David gave strict instructions that Absalom was to be taken alive. But Absalom, mounted on a terrified mule, was caught in the low branches of an oak tree. David's men came upon him, bleeding and wounded. They killed him, buried him in a pit, and covered the body with stones. David's lament, "Absalom, Absalom, my son, Absalom", is well known. Only parents can really understand his agony of mind, when he was told the news. This story is told in the 2nd Book of Samuel.

But let us return to David and his feelings of utter loneliness and misery in the wilderness. Twice it had happened . . . the four thousand feet of barren mountain side with its jagged rocks, its sultry heat, its lack of vegetation, its clefts and hazards, possibly its snakes and vultures . . . what a place! David the poet, David the shepherd, thought about all this in his agony of mind. He imagined himself leading sheep through this awful landscape. He composed words of poetry . . . "The Lord is my shepherd. I shall not want . . . Yea, though I walk through the valley of the shadow I will fear no evil: for thou art with me; thy rod and thy staff they comfort me." This was the deepest, most horrible valley in the whole wide world.

David's first period of sorrow had ended at a place called Engedi. This is a holiday resort today, but surely it is in a most extraordinary position for holiday-making! It is on the banks of the Dead Sea, deep in the bowls of the earth. Above and around it there is the barren mountain side, and before it there are the thick sulphurous waters of the lake. Yet it is a place of great beauty. Fed by the clear rippling water of underground springs, it is a lovely oasis, with trees and shrubs and rich grasslands. David wrote: "He maketh me to lie down in green pastures: he leadeth me beside the still waters." He was thinking of Engedi, of his reconciliation with King Saul.

This, the story of how the 23rd Psalm came to be written, came to me in a strange way. I was in trouble. My wife was seriously ill in hospital. I had two small children, and a job to sustain. My father was dying of cancer in a hospital two hundred miles away. I did somehow manage to get to him and pay my final respects before he died. It was my valley of the shadow. I went through his effects after it was all over – and I found this story! My father's words, unlike his physical self, lived on.

The 23rd Psalm has brought comfort to millions in every generation. I used it once as a theme in a small chapel in the mountains of Snowdonia. A worshipper told me afterwards how she had gone through such a 'valley', over some family matter. She had been sick with worry, but then, one day, as she went in through her gateway she had seen a piece of screwed-up paper, which she picked up. On it, in a schoolchild's writing, in Welsh, she found the words of the 23rd Psalm. It brought her great comfort. The words were from the four-hundred-ycar-old Morgan Bible, which has meant so much to so many generations of Welsh people. Today, coinciding with the four hundredth anniversary of the original, a new Welsh Bible has been published. It is the result of twenty or thirty years of dedicated scholastic work. It reflects great credit on the Rev. Owen E. Evans and his necessarily small team of experts. I interviewed Mr. Evans on my weekly Hospital Radio programme about what will undoubtedly be known in fifty years' time as the 'Owen Evans' Bible'. My thirteen year old 'engineer', Menna Thomas, revealed that she had especially asked her parents for a copy of the bible as a birthday present; Mr. Evans at once offered to autograph it. All this came across spontaneously while we were 'on the air'!

Welsh is an ancient and beautiful language with a rich literary heritage, spoken today by some half a million people. Surprisingly, nearly seventy thousand copies of the new bible have been sold at the time of writing this book!

42. ANOTHER OLDIE

I turn now to Psalm 84.

Verses 6 and 7 read: "Blessed is the man whose strength is in thee . . . Who, passing through the valley of Baca make it a well; the rain also filleth the pools." The meaning is not exactly clear. Young's literal translation reads: "Those passing through a valley of weeping, a fountain do make it." Again, the meaning is not clear. But I *think* it is a beautiful little potted parable.

Although the Hebrew word used here for "valley" is different, I think this takes the 23rd Psalm one stage further. We think of the person deep in trouble, and the Good Shepherd guiding him. Here again we have somebody going through the valley of weeping. It is hot, sultry, his feet are sore, his body is clammy, the valley hems him in on every side; he feels that the journey will never end. He longs for water, so that he can drink and bathe his body.

But being a godly man, he thinks to himself: "Others will come this way. Others will suffer as I am suffering. I know what I'll do! I'll dig a well, or a dewpond, so that they will be able to relieve their discomfort." There is your parable.

It reminds me of a story. Fifty years ago, Christian people, worried about the falling off in church attendances, believed that the cinema was the answer they were looking for. Millions visited the cinema every week. So if they offered films with an evangelical message in churches, the people would come flocking back! The Methodists built their great Central Halls in the inner cities: the Anglicans established an organisation called "The Dawn Trust", with a library of suitable films for hire. In charge of the latter, based in Bournemouth, was a brilliant middle-aged clergyman called Brian Hession.

Then, one day, it happened! Brian Hession discovered that he had a massive rampant internal cancer. They operated, but with little hope.

His natural reaction would have been to ask: "Why, when I am doing all this good work, should this happen to me?" He could have become bitter. Frequently, that is the human response in the face of misfortune, even amongst Christian people. I have known some who have given up all their good works at such a time. They have even turned against their religion! But Brian Hession's faith went deeper than that. He did not question God's will. He said to himself, with the psalmist: "Others will come this way. I must try to make it easier for them."

He created an organisation called "Cancer Anonymous". Its aim was to bring comfort to sufferers, by writing to them and sending them presents, He spoke messages of Christian comfort on tapes, which he lent around. He wrote books. Their titles are self-explanatory . . . *The Gentle Step, Determined to Live*, and others. He poured out the Christian message of courage, trust, peace and faith, with the professional understanding of the trained Minister. Then he died. His organisation survived him by a few years.

This was, surely, greater work than anything he ever did with films; but it would have only been possible to one who was himself in the valley. It could not have been undertaken from outside.

If we have to face up to difficulty, perhaps we have a similar opportunity to turn evil to good purpose. In particular, widows and widowers who know about bereavement can perhaps turn to counselling others as they in turn face up to the loss of loved ones. Paradoxically they may even help themselves in the process.

43. LINK ROAD

The Authorised Version tells us that Psalm 34 is "A Psalm of David, when he changed his behaviour before Abimelech; who drove him away, and he departed". I had to look this up, but even when I had found the incident referred to I did not feel sufficiently inspired by it to want to burst into song!

The psalms, in their original Hebrew, were beautiful indeed. But to the modern Christian their purpose is often obscure. Their doctrine is pre-Christian and, sometimes, unsound. That is why we sing "Glory be to the Father, and to the Son, and to the Holy Spirit . . ." at the end; it is to remind us that this is only the Old Testament. Their translation into English is often quite appalling, whether it be in the biblical form or in the form of doggerel verse. Psalm 150 gives us a flavour of what they were like originally. It lists the instruments that were used in the orchestras that accompanied the singers . . . the trumpet, the lute, the harp, tambourines, flute and strings, and cymbals . . . let everything that hath breath praise the Lord! It mentions dancing; David the king danced in an ephod at one exciting moment during his life. It makes our worship look extremely dull. These songs were in haunting rhythmic poetry, far more stimulating than our 'Common Metre'. So very often, we sing the psalms today with little understanding – and is it surprising?

Anyway, let me illustrate the use of the psalms through the story of the Ark of the Covenant. During the forty years of wandering in the wilderness Moses came down from Mount Sinai, 'from the Lord's presence', bearing God's Laws (Exodus 34:29 onward). He told the Children of Israel that they were to construct a tent, which would be the symbol of God's presence with them. They were also to make various devices for use in worship, and they were to make the sacred 'Ark of the Covenant'. This latter is described at the beginning of Exodus 37. The dimensions were to be roughly four feet by two feet by two feet, winged creatures were to face each other across the lid and there was to be provision for carrying-poles. Acacia wood embellished with gold was to be used. It was to contain the stone tablets, the Commandments, and was to be kept in the sacred tent.

Some five hundred years later David became king over a people who were by now established within the Promised Land. He captured Jerusalem from the Jebusites, and determined to make it, not merely a capital city, but God's Holy City set upon a hill top. Meanwhile the Ark had been abandoned and rediscovered in the woods of Ephraim. Of course it must be conveyed, with proper ceremonial and formality, to this new city.

During the journey, one of the attendants, Uzzah, touched the Ark . . . and fell dead! This must be a judgement from God! They had done something wrong! They hastily moved the Ark into the nearby home of Edom's servant. They waited for three months. Then, gingerly, they moved the Ark six paces . . . and nothing happened. God's anger had been assuaged.

This sequence of events is described in Psalm 30. "I cried to thee, O Lord; and unto the Lord I made supplication" (v. 8). "I cried unto thee, and thou hast healed me" (v. 2). "His anger endureth but a moment . . . weeping may endure for a night, but joy cometh in the morning" (v. 5). "Thou hast turned for me my mourning into dancing . . ." (v. 11).

Eventually the procession arrived at the foot of the mountain. Here Psalm 24 takes over, the psalm which we often use at Harvest Festival time! We have two choirs singing. "Who shall ascend into the hill of the Lord . . . ?" (v. 3) is answered by "He that hath clean hands and a pure heart . . . " (vs. 4 and 5). They reach the top. "Lift up your heads, O ye gates . . . and the King of Glory shall come in" (v. 7). The response comes from inside the city: "Who is this King of Glory?" . . . and the reply: "The Lord strong and mighty, the Lord mighty in battle" (v. 8). This question and answer sequence is repeated in a glorious crescendo. The Ark is carried into the city.

The first ten verses of Psalm 132 represent a kind of recapitulation, a recollection of David's anxieties. "I will not give sleep to mine eyes . . . until I find out a place for the Lord . . . " (vs. 4 and 5). "Lo, we heard of it at Ephratah: we found it in the fields of the wood" (v. 6). "Arise, O Lord, into thy rest; thou, and the ark of thy strength" (v. 8).

The sequence of song concludes with Psalm 101. King David must now dedicate himself to God's service. "I will behave myself wisely in a perfect way . . . " (v. 2). "I will set no wicked thing before mine eyes . . . " (v. 3). "Whoso privily slandereth his neighbour, him will I cut off . . . " (v. 5). "I will destroy all the wicked of the land; that I may cut off all wicked doers from the city of the Lord" (concluding verse).

We sing the psalms in our services – but how far do we really understand what we are singing? Let us return now to the New Testament.

44. BACK TO THE STATION

So let us jump in time now, through many centuries, back again to the old walled town of Southampton. The year is 1694, The Independents by then had a chapel of their own, just outside the walls, on the site of what is now Marks and Spencers' store. Isaac Watts lived at home until 1696, and was a regular attender. The story goes that he was bitterly critical of the quality of the singing and the music, which by tradition had to be based on 'God's word', that is, the psalms that we have just been studying. He could see that everything about them was wrong, the understanding, the theology, the musical rendering, and the crude English metric verse. He voiced his complaint to his father, who suggested that, if that was how he felt, he should try to produce something better. He wrote the hymn "Behold the glories of the Lamb", in Common Metre, This was the start. In 1700 his brother Enoch wrote to him. In essence he issued a challenge. His long letter included the words: "I have been persuaded to a great while since, that were David to speak English, he would choose to make use of your style." The letter is an important piece of history.

Enoch was aware of his brother's 'talent', and wanted to see it used to the full. It took seven years for the idea to come to fruition. Then, in 1707, Isaac Watts published the first English hymn book worthy of the name. It was called *Hymns and Spiritual Songs* (from Ephesians 5:19). It contained two hundred beautiful hymns, some of which have rarely been surpassed in their brilliant inspiration. Some, like "O God (or 'Our God' in the original) our Help in ages past", were based directly on psalms (No. 90). Others used the word 'Jesus' instead of God, but were otherwise based on psalms ("Jesus shall reign" is inspired on Psalm 22). "I'll praise my maker while I've breath" is inspired by Psalm 146, but the next two lines, "And when my voice is lost in death, Praise shall employ my nobler powers", are clearly New Testament. He was well aware that chapel-goers were (and indeed, can be today!) very conservative. But he pointed out that his hymns were really just psalms in modern form (and surely nobody was going to object to the use of the word "Jesus" instead of "God"!). His works were eventually accepted by the traditionally-minded worshippers. Their worship was enriched immeasurably. He took over the whole Independent hymn book.

In or around that same year, 1707, a clergyman's wife in eastern England gave birth to a sickly child, her eighteenth, who was not expected to survive. He did survive; and Charles Wesley, in his later life, with his 6,500 or so hymns, took up the challenge where Watts had left off. Susanna Wesley, the mother, was quite unique among women. Many others have borne a famous son or daughter; but I doubt if any other woman in history has borne *two* such famous sons as John and Charles. Other great hymn writers followed. English hymnology, which today is an established part of the worship of Christians in every corner of the globe, had been well and truly established.

1707 was indeed an important year in English church history!

And we are back at Central Station. God be with you till we meet again!

AFTERMATH

Preacher wrote about his experiences during those seven excursions in the modern City of God, in the hope that others might be able to read his words, and that they might prove helpful.

But, of course, this was not the end. Having been lifted up, he never returned to the depths, although like other Christians he had his moments of doubt and depression. He became a permanent resident in the City, learning more and more about it all the time.

He has always enjoyed meeting people of other nationalities and cultures. His contacts from time to time have been world wide, Americans and Germans, Colombians and Singaporians, Lebanese and Afrikaners – the list is endless. He tries to be "all things to all men" aiming at least to be moderate, intellectually honest, ready always to listen as well as to speak (the attitude St. Paul was advocating). Religious fanaticism, as the non-religious so frequently tell us, is at the root of half the world's troubles.

Shortly after completing his account he had a fascinating contact, with a person who had rejected all forms of religion. She was a lady of great charm and intelligence, an English-speaking Russian, and proud to be a member of the Communist Party. She attended a service at a lively Methodist Church, listening closely to what was said – one wonders if the man conducting the service had any inkling of what was going on in the mind of one of those present. Obviously both Capitalism and Communism are flawed in the eyes of the true Christian. Preacher talked at great length to the lady. He accepted that the Russian Orthodox Church had been, at the time of the Revolution, a bastion of privilege, and that its practices had been remote from the gospel story. But what of the Baptists? She challenged him. "Why, then, has God not made the story of His Son known to all mankind?" Preacher could not answer; he does not always understand the mind of the Creator. They arrived at the point of fundamental difference: she believed in human self-sufficiency, while he believed that we have to be lifted up out of ourselves as St. Paul was on the Damascus Road. He described St. Paul's experience, but, like those men of Athens, she was not convinced. They agreed to differ. "God bless," he said, as they parted, then corrected himself – the familiar phrase was meaningless to her. He used the story of the encounter as a sermon.

Preacher realised, as we must all come to realise, that we cannot 'prove' Christianity. We know, within ourselves, that it *is* a reality. Paul, in his first epistle, addressed to the Thessalonians, wrote: "And the very God of peace sanctify you wholly. I pray God your whole spirit and soul and body be preserved blameless . . . " (Ch. 5:23). Here we have a sort of trinity which exists within ourselves. The body is the physical framework in which we live. The soul is that part of us which cannot be seen. And the spirit is what guides us. In a believer the human spirit forms a link with the Holy Spirit which with the Father and the Son makes up the Godhead in all its wonder. The Holy Spirit helps him with his prayers, intervenes in his affairs, gives him wisdom in distinguishing right from wrong. All this is abundantly true, a matter of repeated experience . . . but it can only be conveyed to one who is willing to try for himself. This text and theme was used in a famous sermon preached by the great but tragic Frederick W. Robertson at Trinity Church, Brighton, on Trinity Sunday, 1850. Preacher adapted it, using Romans 8:26 – end, Luke 6:1-11, and relevant hymns, as his illustrations. The service was one of those rare and wonderful occasions when from beginning to end everybody obviously sensed the presence of the Holy Spirit – but that was because they were all believing Christians.

And here we really must stop. Sunday by Sunday Preacher finds fresh inspiration. He improves on existing themes, with better readings and better hymns. He gets new ideas. And the story goes on and on and on.

Eventually, like Bunyan's pilgrims, Christian and Hopeful, he will have to make the fearful crossing to the other side, to find the heavenly Jerusalem, the paradise of God. Like Isaac Watts he must, timorous mortal that he is, cross the swelling flood to reach that land of pure delight. Already he has glimpsed the countryside beyond as he gazed across the waters from the city. He has, if you like, seen the Jersey coastline from a Manhattan skyscraper. Now he will find it, the beginnings of a continent of unlimited dimensions, indescribable, quite beyond human imagination. If he passes muster this will be his joyful home in timeless eternity.

AUTHOR'S NOTE. RETURN TO NEW YORK

This book has been based figuratively on New York. No other city in the world would have suited my purpose; New York is an extraordinary place. Manhattan is a rocky island twelve miles long and two miles wide, criss-crossed by vertical Avenues and horizontal Streets, with the open expanse of Central Park at its centre. Beneath the surface there is a network of Subway and Railway lines. Above ground the modern buildings rise up to a height of a thousand feet or more; there is nothing to compare with it anywhere. Grand Central Station is at its heart, a pre-Great-War architectural masterpiece in its own right, with the magnificent Pan Am Building reaching to the heavens above its platforms.

The City's symbol is the Statue of Liberty. Present-day New Yorkers speak with emotion about their ancestors who arrived penniless, and whose first sight of the statue as they entered the harbour told them that they were at last in the land of freedom and opportunity.

I first visited New York in 1943. I was a naval officer, and arrived at Pier 90 in the 80,000 ton liner *Queen Elizabeth*. I had by then experienced plenty of the absurd tragedy of action at sea. I had come from dismal blacked-out Britain, with its air raids and shortages. New York was paradise! It was not just the bright lights and the prosperity. It was the generosity and kindness of the people which left such a lasting impression. It was indescribable. When eventually I found myself serving in the Atlantic convoy that was to take me back into war at sea I had acquired a love of all things American. It remains with me to this day!

I had found warm Christian fellowship in a small Methodist Church near Central Park, which drew its mainly Swedish congregation from the suburbs. In 1989 I returned. Back in the same Lexington United Methodist Church I found it had changed surprisingly little (in fact the picture on the front of the service sheet was still the same). The elderly gentleman welcoming the worshippers at the door told me, incredibly, that he remembered me! Of course there were now many younger people in the church. But a small group of older people had been attending since well before 1943. There was a rare atmosphere of Christian sincerity in the worship. The Minister's welcome to 'David Irons, who drops in every forty-five years or so' attracted restrained applause!

Unfortunately, television delights in concentrating on the seedier side of present-day New York life. The city does have obvious problems. But during my recent stay, having visited the magnificent Episcopalian Cathedral and seen something of Methodist organisation on a grand scale, I realised that there is another side never shown on television. New York is a city in which Christianity, my Christianity, is vibrantly alive, fit and well.

David Irons
"Bryn Hyfryd"
Llansadwrn
MENAI BRIDGE
Gwynedd
LL59 5SN
U.K.